The Complete Guide to Selling Your Home

The Complete Guide to Selling Your Home

Michael C. Thomsett

DOW JONES-IRWIN
Homewood, Illinois 60430

This publication is designed to provide accurate and authoritative information in regard to the subject matter covered. It is sold with the understanding that neither the author nor the publisher is engaged in rendering legal, accounting, or other professional service. If legal advice or other expert assistance is required, the services of a competent professional person should be sought.

From a Declaration of Principles jointly adopted by a Committee of the American Bar Association and Committee of Publishers.
Acquisitions editor: Richard A. Luecke
Project editor: Joan A. Hopkins
Production manager: Ann Cassady
Jacket designer: Image House
Compositor: Caliber Design Planning, Inc.
Typeface: 11/13 Times Roman
Printer: Arcata Graphics/Kingsport

Library of Congress Cataloging-in-Publication Data

Thomsett, Michael C.
  The complete guide to selling your home.

  Includes index.
  1. House selling—United States. 2. Real estate business—United States. I. Title.
HD1379.T46 1989   333.33'8   88–15025
ISBN 1-55623-123-7

Printed in the United States of America
1 2 3 4 5 6 7 8 9 0 K 5 4 3 2 1 0 9 8

For Linda, Eric, and Mike

CONTENTS

SECTION 3
After the Sale

SECTION 1

PREPARING
FOR THE SALE

CHAPTER 1

REASONS TO SELL YOUR HOME

If you are planning to sell your home, you have a number of important decisions to make, such as choosing a broker, setting your price, getting the property into marketable shape, and moving. You must also prepare for the disruption of buyers walking through and critically examining your personal shelter.

In this book, a methodical approach to help you make the decisions you will face throughout the selling process is suggested. The greatest chance for errors results from lack of careful and complete research. So before you put a sign on your front lawn, and before you call a real estate broker, plan to examine the market, your house, and your neighborhood.

Real estate has proven to be one of the most profitable and dependable investments over time. The demand for housing is a constant; property values grow because of that demand. But because the supply and demand change from one time to another, and from one area to another, you must understand the market before you place your house for sale.

At one point in the supply and demand cycle, the demand will be low and prices will lag as a result. At another point, buyer demands will exceed the supply of homes, and the value of your property will increase. These conditions are also affected by interest rates, income taxes, the local unemployment rate, new businesses coming into your area, proximity to large cities, and a number of other economic factors. You will see how all of these conditions affect how and when you sell your house, and what you can expect once you become a seller.

The first of the three sections in this book examines the many aspects of preparing for the sale. You will learn how to evaluate your property, and how to make a decision about the best way to get the price you want. Only after defining the market and deciding on a price should you actually enter the selling process. In the second section, we'll discuss brokers and what you should expect from them, whether or not you should attempt to sell on your own, and the special problems of selling in a slow market. In the last section, issues that come up after the sale—income taxes, deferral of profits, and buying a new home—are explored.

Perhaps the most important decision you will have to make is where you will live after the sale. People sell their homes for a variety of reasons. One may be to "take the profit out" of an appreciated house. But remember that when you sell, you still have to live somewhere. As long as you continue to need shelter, you probably will not realize actual profits. You will only reinvest them in another home.

Before proceeding with all of the details of your sale, examine and eliminate the alternatives. By removing any doubt that selling your home is your wisest personal and financial decision prior to beginning the process, you will be able to proceed with complete confidence. First, make a clear distinction between investment and personal property. When you invest money, you hope for appreciation in the future; but as a homeowner, you are more concerned with the quality of the property and the neighborhood, convenience, room sizes, and other personal concerns. As you make the transition from owner to seller, you certainly want the best price for your home, but you must evaluate your motives for placing your property on the market.

PERCEPTIONS OF MARKET VALUE

When real estate prices go up in an area, there is always a rash of "selling fever." Owners want to take their profits before prices go back down. But when prices are up for your home, they are also up for other real estate. So the next house you buy will probably reflect the same amount of increased value. Rather than taking out your profit, you only reinvest it elsewhere.

EXAMPLE:

Suppose you bought your home when the average residence in the area was selling for $85,000. Today, your home is worth approximately $125,000. You can make a $40,000 profit before commissions and closing costs. But when you investigate the surrounding market for other homes, you discover you will have to reinvest at least $125,000 in another property. In this situation, moving disrupts your family's life *and* costs money. Besides the closing costs you will pay, first as a seller and then as a buyer, you must pay for moving your belongings. You will also experience the inconveniences of changing your address, moving children to a new school, and leaving neighbors who have become good friends.

If you are thinking of moving primarily because you want to take the profit out of your home, first investigate prices in your area. If you will have to reinvest all of your proceeds, you are not really taking out your profit, just making an expensive change.

MOVING TO A NEW AREA

Some people sell because they need or want to move to a different area. For instance, your employer offers you a transfer and will pay your moving expenses. Even if this involves a promotion and career opportunity, you must evaluate whether the move will be a wise one, and whether or not you can afford the move.

EXAMPLE:

Ted and his family live in Fargo, North Dakota, where they own a three-bedroom home valued at about $90,000. Ted's employer, a branch office of a large company, has offered him a transfer to the New York City office. He will be promoted and given a 20 percent pay raise, and the opportunity is a promising one. But upon investigating the price of housing, Ted discovers that a comparable home within 100 miles of New York will cost $250,000 or more.

This dilemma is faced every year by thousands of people who relocate from areas where real estate prices are modest. Since a large number of transfers are from small areas to major metropolitan areas, chances are that property is very much in demand and that values change more rapidly than in less populated regions. Real estate prices in and around New York, Boston, southern California, and San Francisco—four of the best career markets—are among the highest in the United States today. If you move from a suburban midwestern or northeastern city, you must expect a shock when you compare real estate values.

Most first-time homeowners keep their property for less than five years. That's not enough time to build up a lot of equity in a home, especially if paying on a 30-year mortgage. If, for example, the interest rate on your mortgage is 10 percent, you have only paid off about 3.5 percent of your mortgage balance by the end of the fifth year. So any profits will have to come from increased market value of the property itself. If your move is to an area where prices are equal to or higher than where you live now, you will not realize a profit from moving.

THE SOLUTION:

> If you are offered a transfer or are considering a job offer from an employer in a different city, investigate the real estate market in that area. You can ask for help from a real estate brokerage firm with offices in your city and in the area you're considering moving to. Ask these questions:
>
> 1. Would you describe today's conditions as a buyer's market (where ample properties are available) or a seller's market (where demand is greater than the supply of homes)? The level of supply and demand will affect prices and the amount of choice you have in picking a home in a desirable area.
> 2. During the last two years, what was the average sales price of homes comparable to mine, located in similar neighborhoods?
> 3. What are the average annual salaries for people in my occupation?
> 4. How does the area compare in terms of schools, safety, population, and other attributes that will affect my family?

You are at a real disadvantage when you have to depend on a real estate broker to answer these questions. If you do not know the area well, it is always desirable to visit personally and look around for yourself. Even with the best of intentions, no one else can tell you about the flavor of an area, the quality of life, or how economic conditions compare.

If your current or prospective employers are serious about a relocation, they should be willing to pay for an investigative trip. Visit the new area, check home prices and salary levels, look around neighborhoods, and see for yourself what kind of living conditions to expect. Read the want ads thoroughly, comparing house prices and salary levels to your present area. This will give you a good idea of how the two locations generally compare, both in terms of the economy and of the environment.

MOVING TO A LARGER HOME

Another popular reason to move is because a family has outgrown its present home. This may be due to an increase in your family's size and a need for more space, or because you simply want to upgrade your standard of living as you begin to earn more money.

An alternative to moving is adding on to your home. If you are satisfied with the neighborhood and enjoy the convenience of your location, you might save money and avoid disruption by increasing your living space rather than replacing it.

If you are considering moving to another area where property values have increased on a par with those in your own neighborhood, chances are you will lose rather than profit from the move. And if interest rates are higher now than when you signed your mortgage, you will end up with a higher monthly payment. Improving on what you now own could be a smart solution.

Without changing the terms of a mortgage that you think has a favorable rate, consider financing an improvement with a home equity loan. This allows you to upgrade the quality of you home *and* its value. You solve your space problem without uprooting your family and moving to a new neighborhood.

RENTING OUT YOUR PROPERTY

Before concluding that it is time to sell your home, there is one last alternative: continuing as the owner and renting it to someone else. While this might seem practical at first glance, it has a negative side. If you will be moving to another city or state, you will have to manage the property from a distance or depend on someone else to represent you. In either case, you are at a disadvantage. There is no substitute for being able to personally check your property every week or two and deal directly with a tenant.

If you have never been a landlord, you must be prepared for the risks that go with this venture. First, your tenant might not pay rent in time for you to make your mortgage payments, or you might never receive full payment. Second, you have no assurance that the tenant will take good care of your house, keeping the landscaping in order and respecting the walls, floors, and carpeting. Third, depending on the demand for rentals, you might not be able to keep the house occupied every month. And finally, what initially appears to be a simple and financially sound move could end up disrupting your personal life. Tenants might call at all hours of the day and night, including weekends, to demand repairs. As an owner, you took care of those recurring repairs on your own, or put them off until you could afford them. But tenants expect an immediate response, and want the property kept in perfect working order at all times.

These potential problems are the price you pay for keeping a house as a rental unit. In an ideal situation, your tenant will care for your property and pay rent on time, perhaps even paying for maintenance. The rent will cover your mortgage payments and any repairs that are needed. And after many years, you will own the house free and clear, and it will have appreciated in market value.

In many states, a reduction in property taxes is allowed to owners who occupy their homes. So renting out your property could increase your tax expenses. This must be kept in mind when you estimate whether or not you can make a profit by renting your house.

Many people have had enjoyable and rewarding experiences as landlords; others have regretted it. Check the laws and regulations in your area regarding rent control, tenants' rights, and landlord responsibilities. Be sure you enter into a landlord situation with complete knowledge about the legal restrictions and obligations under which you must operate. Also be prepared to screen potential tenants carefully, including contact with previous landlords. And be aware that a landlord's life is not necessarily free of worry.

As we have discussed, there are three general reasons for selling: to take out profits, to move to a new area, or to increase living space. You might want to take profits merely because values have gone up, or to liquidate ownership because of a divorce or the death of your spouse. A move often is connected to a job promotion or complete job change. And if your family is growing, you may need to increase your living area. These three motives could be resolved without actually selling. The reasons, problems, and possible solutions are summarized in Figure 1–1.

THE DECISION TO MOVE

Once you have eliminated the alternatives and concluded that selling is, in fact, your best move, you are ready to evaluate your property and put it on the market. At this point, you cease to think of your home as a personal asset and begin to consider its market value. You will identify needed repairs and improvements that will increase market value and attract potential buyers, study the market in your area to estimate what you can expect to receive for your home, and look for a real estate broker.

Some guidelines to keep in mind as you begin this process follow:
1. Remember that the current market value of your home will be

FIGURE 1–1
Alternatives to Selling Your Home

REASON	PROBLEM	SOLUTION
to take profits	profits must be reinvested	compare personal versus investment values
to move to a new area	you lack information	get the facts before making a decision
to increase living space	other property values might be higher	become a landlord
		add on to your home
	interest rates are higher now	

determined by the level of demand for housing in your area. If a lot of homes are for sale and buyers are scarce, the price will be driven down; if the reverse is true, your home should sell quickly at or near your asked price.

2. A second factor affecting market value will be recent sales prices of similar homes in your area. The level of care and maintenance, the amount spent on improvements, and the quality of workmanship and materials in your home are all important factors. But they are, in fact, secondary to the "going rate" for homes like yours.

3. Your flexibility as a seller might affect how fast your home is actually sold. Buyers often make offers below your asking price, on the assumption that you are asking more than you actually want. Your home will sell more quickly if you are willing to negotiate. If you are firm about the price, you must expect a delay in completing the sale—assuming that there are other homes for sale in approximately the same price range. However, when there are many more buyers than sellers, you will probably get a fast offer, and at the price you want. In the most extreme buyer's market, you could even get offers *above* your asked price.

These issues are covered in greater detail in upcoming chapters. But as you begin the process of placing your home on the market, it is important to be aware of these realities beforehand. The next chapter explains methods of evaluating your home, both for its reasonable market value and for its readiness and market appeal.

CHAPTER 2

EVALUATING YOUR PROPERTY

The first step most people take when they want to sell their home is contacting a real estate broker. The broker visits the house and arrives at a general estimate of market value. The broker might also suggest improvements or cosmetic changes the homeowner should make to increase the appeal of the property to prospective buyers. This is the *usual* way a seller places a home on the market. But it is not the best way. There are several flaws in this method.

THE CONDITION OF YOUR HOUSE

Contacting a broker first is a mistake. Many preparatory steps should be taken well in advance of bringing in a broker, who is an expert at marketing a property. Why? Because the broker must judge how readily the property can be matched with a buyer, and serves as a specialist in helping people sell their homes. While you will probably want to use the services of a broker once your home is ready for sale, you should first evaluate it as it now stands and figure out how to make it more appealing—before you bring the sales expert into the picture.

Another flaw in this method is the way in which brokers are chosen. Most sellers pick a broker randomly. They often go to the nearest real estate office and speak with the broker who is available at that moment. This is a hit-or-miss method at best. At worst, you will get the least busy person in the office—perhaps the most recently hired and most inexperienced real estate salesperson in that company.

To get the best representation and, ultimately, the best price and terms for your sale, you should shop around for a broker, asking the right questions and following up on referrals from knowledgeable people. Methods of shopping for brokers are explained in Chapter 10.

When a broker comes to the seller's house, he or she looks at the property inside and out, and might even invite other agents and brokers for what is called a "walk-through." They offer opinions of reasonable market value and will probably suggest changes to prepare the house for presentation. These might include simple landscaping (mowing the lawn and trimming the hedges), painting the outside, inside, or both, or replacing cracked windows. (A checklist of fixing-up expenses is included in Chapter 9.)

These suggestions usually relate to things you already are aware of as an owner—repairs you put off or simply accept and live with. But when buyers are shown a property, these little details tend to make a very poor overall impression. The offers you receive will be lower when basic maintenance has been ignored. Real estate brokers and agents, aware of this fact, encourage would-be sellers to take these steps, at a minimum, before showing the property.

You certainly can take care of such details on your own before contacting a real estate broker. But there is another reason to prepare your home prior to getting in touch with brokers. Their first impressions from the general appearance of your home will make them draw certain conclusions. If a broker believes your house will be harder to sell than another one down the block, he or she will suggest that you lower your price a few thousand dollars because minor flaws are visible, even though they could be fixed relatively easily.

Start thinking like a seller. Before inviting a real estate broker into your home, take the steps to put the property into good shape, so the broker will be eager to bring buyers through and show it off. If you make the broker's selling job an easy one, you are more likely to get the price you want, or a price close to it.

THE AGE OF YOUR HOME

Old homes, as a general rule, were built to a higher standard of construction and better workmanship. In many areas of the country, building codes are more liberal today than in the past. This is especially true when demand has grown at a rapid rate, while the cost of construction has increased significantly. So an older home, just on the basis of the quality of construction, should command a higher market price.

However, this is not a positive factor in reality. The demand for brand-new homes is generally higher than for older ones. The assembly-line approach to house building that occurs in the tracts in many rapidly expanding regions does not seem to concern the modern buyer. Many assume that older homes come with expensive problems hidden in plumbing, electrical, and other behind-the-wall systems. These assumptions are not always true, and they can be protected against with a thorough professional home inspection (see Chapter 7). But even if you include warranties and stress the quality of your home's construction, a large segment of the buying population simply wants a house that has not been lived in by anyone else.

If you are placing an older home on the market—even if it's only 10 or 15 years old—and you will be competing with a newly built tract development nearby, you face several disadvantages:

1. A tract developer sells in volume. A large number of buyers are "processed" in a relatively short period of time. In sheer volume alone, the developer has an advantage over the seller of a single property.
2. The availability of several models gives buyers a choice. For a difference of a few thousand dollars, a buyer can select a specific home ideally suited to his needs.
3. If selling is done through models before the actual home is built, the buyer can often negotiate customized changes to a tract home for a relatively small additional fee.
4. The developer might assist with financing, making it easier for first-time buyers to qualify, or offer an attractively low rate through agreement with a lender, or sell units for a low down payment.

How do you compete with these features? Not only are the homes new (often coming with one-year warranties), but the developer does all he or she can to sell units quickly and conveniently. In this situation, you must evaluate your home both in terms of its condition and the competition. You might decide to lower your price to attract buyers who will otherwise follow the crowd to a new development.

Your decision depends on the level of demand for homes. If your area is expanding and the need is greater than the demand, you will have no problem finding a buyer. But if the market is slow, you should consider lowering your price, even when that huge tract is not going up.

Your task—determining the fair market value of your home based on the current demand—is especially difficult when the market is slow and tracts are developing anyway. While a high volume of new residential development usually indicates an increase in demand, it is not always the case. Development often surpasses the height of the demand cycle. The supply and demand cycle in real estate is difficult to track because actual trends never move in straight lines; rather, temporary ups and downs make it impossible to know exactly what part of the cycle we are in at any given moment (see Figure 2–1).

In retrospect, a predictable pattern can be seen. At the low point of the demand swing, there is an excess of available homes, and construction is minimal. As demand increases, construction activity picks up, and new housing is created. Then the demand peaks, and begins to decline,

FIGURE 2–1
The Supply and Demand Cycle

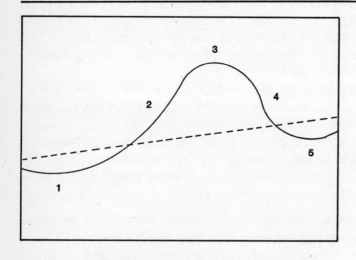

1 demand is at a low

2 demand increases, construction
  volume grows in response

3 demand peaks

4 construction continues as
  demand falls

5 demand is at a low, construction
  volume falls

---- long–term appreciation of
     real estate

but construction activity continues, perhaps even increasing. This phase continues until the excess of available homes creates a glut. Demand has again fallen to its lowest point, and only then will construction activity cease.

Throughout the swings in supply and demand, real estate values continue to grow in a steady but gradual line. Over the long term (periods of 20 to 50 years or more), the value of owner-occupied homes matches and usually surpasses the Consumer Price Index. According to the National Association of REALTORS®, housing prices for the 15 years ending in 1980 exceeded the rate of inflation for the same period by 2 percent overall.

YOUR NEIGHBORHOOD AS A FACTOR

As a seller, you must be prepared to offer a price that is right for four conditions:

1. The level of supply and demand.
2. The condition and features of the house itself.
3. Recent sales prices of similar properties in the same area.
4. The neighborhood.

Why does a neighborhood have so much to do with a house's market value? Two properties that are exactly the same could be very different in price—often by $100,000 or more. It all depends on the location. Some neighborhoods are more desirable because of conveniences, reputation, level of crime, and other factors. Even within a single neighborhood, prices could vary due to:

1. *Amount of traffic noise.* One house on a main thoroughfare is exposed to constant traffic, making it more difficult to sell and probably lowering the market value. An exact duplicate of the house one block removed from the noise and inconvenience could be worth several thousand dollars more.
2. *The view.* Your house might offer a view of a landmark, bridge, a city skyline, an ocean, or a lake. But a neighbor's house that does not have the same view will sell for a much lower price.
3. *Size, shape, and location of the lot.* A corner lot will be viewed as more desirable by some and less desirable by others. A rectangular lot will have a higher value than an oddly shaped one.

To determine whether your home will sell easily at the price you expect, look around your neighborhood. Ask yourself these questions:

1. *Are other homes being well maintained?* Are homeowners mowing lawns, trimming hedges, adding fresh paint, repairing roofs? Is there a sense of pride in ownership among your neighbors?
2. *Are many homes being improved?* When your neighbors are expanding space and making homes more valuable, that's a good sign.
3. *Are zoning laws being enforced?* An area that strictly defines residential areas maintains a higher quality of life.
4. *Is the traffic level controlled?* A smoothly running, well-planned area, free of smog, noise, and congestion is always a more desirable place to live.

Buyers should make the same evaluation when considering a new area. If they look at your area critically, they will make a judgment about whether or not they want to live in your house. As a seller, you should be aware of the positive and negative aspects of your neighborhood before setting a price.

Neighborhoods go through transitions, which can be either positive or negative. You should expect to receive offers below your asked price when transitions are negative. Some signs to look for include:

1. *A large number of homes for sale.* This shows that people are moving away and that buyers can choose from a variety of available properties.
2. *Homes available or vacant for many months.* When properties do not sell quickly, the area is not in demand among buyers. If your area has a number of empty properties, that is a very negative indicator.
3. *Empty lots.* This is a sign that demand for homes is at a low, and that builders and developers do not view the area as worthy of new construction.
4. *Zoning transitions.* Is your neighborhood a mixture of commercial and residential properties? When service stations, fast-food restaurants, motels, and industrial sites begin to operate in a previously residential area, your property value will fall as a result.
5. *High crime level.* Is crime on the rise in your area? If so, the neighborhood is undergoing a negative transition. An increase in

arson fires or fires of suspicious origin should be of special
concern to you. When fire rates increase, properties lose value
and investors cannot easily recapture their investments by selling.

6. *Increasing rate of rentals.* When most of the homes in your area
are occupied not by owners but by renters, turnover of residents
will be higher and the general condition of properties will usually
decline.

SELLERS AND BUYERS

A smart buyer will appraise your neighborhood along these lines. And as
a smart seller, you should make the same evaluation. The majority of
sellers and buyers do not analyze houses or areas in this much depth. As a
result, neither side understands the reasons that a property's value is high
or low, or why a home sells quickly or not at all.

Smart sellers have their facts in hand. Know all of the factors at
work in your area that affect the value of your home, either attracting or
repelling the typical buyer. Prepare yourself well for the process of
selling. Only by knowing in advance whether your home will be in
demand can you logically set a price. A real estate broker can and will
advise you, but it is up to you to decide on an asked price.

Even if the broker hires an independent appraiser, you have the final
word. One person, aware of national trends in housing prices, decided to
sell. He had purchased his home eight years ago for $79,500 and wanted
to sell it for $110,000. The real estate broker recommended a price of
$99,500, but the owner resisted that price. Because the price was ex-
cessively high, no one even made an offer. The seller's mistake was
assuming that values in his area reflected the national average. But while
overall trends might be encouraging from an investor's point of view,
they are meaningless if your home is not appreciating at that rate. Certain
areas experience tremendous demand and skyrocketing prices, while real
estate prices nearby might be falling.

This seller was not aware of the realities in his area. A large number
of homes were for sale, all below his asked price. He was aware of sales
prices of homes in the same county, but did not understand that his
immediate neighborhood mattered more. Other neighborhoods were perceived as better places to live than his part of town.

Another seller had the opposite experience. A broker recommended an asked price of $124,950. But the seller knew that other homes in the same area were selling for $10,000 more. She also knew that many new families were moving to the area, and that there were not enough homes for all of them. It was a seller's market. The seller insisted on a much higher price, and was able to enter a contract within less than a month, getting the full asked price.

Follow these steps to get your facts:

1. *Drive around your neighborhood and look for signs of transition,* both positive and negative.

2. *Speak with the local fire and police departments to get crime and fire statistics.* An increasing trend in personal and property crimes indicates that an area is deteriorating and becoming a less desirable place to live. And if property fires—especially those caused by arson or of a suspicious nature—are on the rise, you know that property values are declining. This is a problem in some areas, primarily with commercial property. But commercial problems often affect residential property values as well.

3. *Check with your savings and loan association or real estate broker for sales trends* for your neighborhood for the last two years. How many homes similar to yours have gone on the market? What was the average asked price, the average sales price, and the number of months those homes were on the market? (Chapter 4 tells how to interpret these statistics.)

Once you know the conditions in your local market, you will be prepared to make an intelligent, informed decision. You will know how much demand there is likely to be for your home, and whether or not your price is realistic. You should also know how long it will take to get a serious offer. By taking these steps you will be in charge, and can proceed as an informed seller who understands the conditions of the market.

THE FIXER-UPPER HOME

Some relatively minor repairs can go a long way toward increasing the market value of your home. Buyers will look for bargains in so-called fixer-upper properties, those that have not been well maintained. As a seller, you must remember that appearance and first impressions are critical to how a buyer will respond. A poorly maintained front yard, an out-of-order doorbell, and chipped paint signal the buyer that the price is too high—even if you have already discounted your asked price because of your home's condition.

If you have major structural or system problems, fixing them will require a major investment. But many of the smaller repairs can be taken care of with only a few hundred dollars and a few hours of your time. Be aware of appearance and take steps to upgrade your home. Make it as presentable as you can.

Minor cosmetic changes aimed at improving the appearance of your property could prove to be impressive investments. It is not unusual for a home's price to increase by twice the amount of money spent repairing it. Just in preparing to show the house, you can change its appearance and status from a fixer-upper to an acceptably well-maintained property.

How does your house look next to the neighboring properties? If other houses are in better shape than yours, a new coat of paint, some landscaping, and replacement of missing shingles can bring your house up to par. If your house looks much better than your neighbor's, that's positive in one respect. But it also speaks poorly for the neighborhood in general. Unfortunately, there is not much that you can do as a seller to improve the impression your neighbors make.

Guidelines for a more detailed evaluation of your home are provided in the following chapter, along with ideas for developing your perspective as a seller.

CHAPTER 3

A SELLER'S PERSPECTIVE

How do you, as a seller, think of the house you are about to put on the market? Don't overlook the fact that, with few exceptions, sellers will soon become buyers again. Once you sell your property, you must find another place to live. Chances are, you play both roles at the same time—purchasing a new home while placing your old home on the market.

VIEWING YOUR HOME AS A BUYER

There are pitfalls when you are under pressure to buy. You probably believe you must realize enough of a profit to achieve three objectives:

1. You must justify the wisdom of buying your first house. What was once shelter for your family now becomes an investment, and should be profitable.
2. You need to take out enough cash after paying off the mortgage and all closing costs to make a down payment on a new home of equal or higher value.
3. The new home must be at least as good an investment as the old one.

This way of thinking is understandable, but it is also a trap for you, as a seller. Remember that the buyer of your home has a certain point of view. She is probably thinking of convenience, location, and price. She is not taking the investor's attitude, and is not as concerned with future value as much as with more immediate needs. And if this is a first purchase, she is not thinking of the three common objectives that sellers have.

You do not need to justify your original purchase, as long as it was right for you and your family at the time. If values have increased since you bought your home, you are only transferring equity, not making a profit. Don't forget your buyer's perspective when you become a seller.

Remember that unless you are given a free house, your home equity is only moved from one place to another. You might be able to afford a more expensive home, even one that will grow in value more rapidly than your previous home. But that should not be a major consideration for you at this point. Of greater concern should be your new home's location, condition, convenience, and price—just like the concerns of the buyer of the home you are selling.

This is not to suggest that profiting from real estate is a negative. In fact, that's how many Americans build most of their personal net worth. Your major savings accumulate over time in your home. But whenever you transfer from one place to another, the motive should be quality of life rather than the bottom line.

A CASE HISTORY:

Tom and Janice Martell bought their first home in a modest tract development. Five years later, they had one child and another on the way. The two-bedroom tract was no longer large enough for them, and they could now afford a more expensive home. It was time to move.

Tom wanted to live in a district where homes were fairly expensive. In fact, the neighborhood was beyond their budget. But, he figured, in a quality neighborhood, prices would increase more rapidly and the house would be a smart investment.

They found a four-bedroom house and made an offer. The lender would carry a maximum of 80 percent of the home's purchase price, with a 15-year variable-rate loan. The couple had enough cash for 10 percent down and closing costs, and they borrowed an additional 10 percent from a relative. It was a strain on their budget, but Tom and Janice were happy with their decision.

A year later, the investment didn't look as good. Many of the homes in the area were for sale. The area was largely supported by a major defense contractor, and thousands of workers had been laid off. People wanted to move. Prices of homes in the Martells' neighborhood fell as sellers became anxious. Buyers made lower offers, not only because a lot of houses were for sale, but because interest rates had risen as well. Many buyers could not qualify for loans at the higher prices these homes used to command.

In the Martells' old neighborhood, where homes were much less expensive, the demand steadily increased. With higher interest rates, these were suddenly bargain properties.

In this case, a prestigious neighborhood enjoyed inflated values as long as the area prospered. But with the combined problems of unemployment and high interest rates, more modestly priced homes proved to be better investments. The Martells realized—too late—that their decision was based on *investment* value, and they had made a poor judgment.

DEFINING VALUE

The supply and demand factor in your area has a lot to do with how easily you will find a buyer and get the price you want for your home. When deciding to sell and then find another place to live, look beyond the rather limited perspective of net profit.

Some sellers become preoccupied with price—the compelling need to sell a home for a higher amount than it was purchased for, and to buy a home that's a better investment value. Suspending your personal priorities, and thinking as an investor while your home is on the market, can affect your decision. Just as this is a mistake the first time you buy, it can also cloud your judgment as a seller.

If you decide you *must* make a profit, you will probably demand too high a price for your home. Competing properties will then move quicker, and your house will remain on the market for many months.

You should consider the other kinds of value you have as a homeowner to help you develop a realistic seller's perspective. Your benefits in owning a home might not all be as obvious as you think. Owners profit in these ways:

1. *With a fixed-rate mortgage, the cost of keeping your house is also fixed.* Your mortgage payment will not change for as long as 30 years. Even with a variable-rate mortgage, the maximum rate of interest is normally fixed within the contract. So there is a ceiling on your cost of housing.

2. *The cost actually decreases over time if you have a fixed-rate mortgage.* As your career progresses, you earn more; with inflation, today's dollar is worth less in the future. Therefore, a fixed monthly payment, over time, becomes a smaller portion of your total income.

EXAMPLE:

In 1965, your family's total monthly income was $2,000. Your mortgage payment was fixed at $166 per month (8.3 percent of income). Twenty years later, your income had risen to $4,500 per month. That same fixed-rate mortgage then represented only 3.7 percent of income.

3. *You decide when to move or how long to stay.* As a renter, your apartment building might be sold, or rents raised too high for you to afford.

4. *To a degree, the value of your property depends on how much care and maintenance you put into it.* You literally tend your investment.

These personal benefits of home ownership surpass the financial gain you may expect upon sale. Keeping these points in mind when evaluating your home purely for its investment value helps you keep your perspective. You are a seller, but will also become a buyer at about the same time. You will move to another home, condominium, or apartment. And the personal values and benefits of ownership should be kept in mind when you make that transition.

IDENTIFYING INVESTMENT VALUE

There is much more to consider in selling your home than simply investment value, although that, too, is an important aspect in deciding to move. You might need to transfer to another area, want a larger home for a growing family, or tire of your neighborhood. But if the decision to move is voluntary, you should estimate the amount of profit you will make.

To determine the investment value of your present home:

1. *Estimate the current value of your home.* Base this on recent sales in the same area of properties similar to yours. If you want a fast sale, reduce your estimate by several thousand dollars, anticipating an offer below your asked price.

2. *Subtract your estimate of closing costs.* The real estate broker's commission will average 6 percent of the sales price. Ask your banker or loan officer for a rough estimate of other sellers' closing costs.

3. *Subtract repairs you expect to make to ready the home for sale,* to fix termite damage or other problems a buyer might point out to you. Your estimate should depend on the age of your home and on how much maintenance you have performed while you owned it.

4. *The balance is your net sales price,* the amount due to you net of commissions, closing costs, and repairs.

5. *Next, figure out the adjusted purchase price of your home.* This consists of your original purchase price, plus closing costs and any improvements you made while you owned the house.

6. *Subtract the adjusted purchase price from the net sales price to estimate profits.* Before proceeding, consider the costs of moving and storage. Reduce your estimated profit by this amount.

7. *The percentage of profit is determined by dividing that profit by the adjusted purchase price.*

8. *The percentage of profit should be divided by the number of years you lived in your home.* This gives you a means for comparison. It is the annual return on your investment.

In a more exact computation, the rate of return would be adjusted by the amount of your original down payment, the number of years you owned the house, the rate of interest you paid, and the tax benefits from deducting interest and property taxes. (See Figure 3–1.) But this computation will suffice to give you a basis for comparing different investments.

As a seller who is about to become a buyer as well, you must look at your annual return on investment in your home and ask several questions:

1. Would you have been better off staying in an apartment and saving money in a passbook account?

FIGURE 3–1
Investment Value

estimated current value	$ _____	
less: closing costs	_____	
repairs	_____	
net sales price	$ _____	
purchase price	$ _____	
plus: closing costs	_____	
improvements	_____	
adjusted purchase price	$ _____	
estimated profit	$ _____	

a)
$$\frac{\text{profit}}{\text{adjusted purchase price}} \quad \frac{\$}{\$} \text{_____} = \text{_____} \% \text{ profit}$$

b)
$$\frac{\% \text{ profit}}{\text{years owned}} \quad \text{_____} \% = \text{_____} \% \text{ annual return}$$

Consider the average level of rents today, versus what they were the last time you lived in an apartment. Also remember that owning your own home has many intangible benefits. This comparison is not really a fair one.

When you rent, you probably will not always invest or save the difference between rent and mortgage payments. The homeowner is, in a sense, forced to build equity by making payments every month.

2. Do you know of other investments that would have yielded a better return on your money?

Chances are, you could earn a higher rate—in hindsight. But keep in mind that most other forms of investment that offer comparable rates of return might also be greater risks. It will be difficult to find an investment that will yield as much as your own home, for as little risk.

3. Do you expect to match the rate of return by investing in another home, or to do better?

Your computation of investment value now takes on real meaning. The purpose of going through the process is to develop a dependable means for evaluation. By comparing rates of return on your home to the same rates in another home you are thinking of buying, you can decide whether that new home is as good an investment.

INTANGIBLE VALUES

Figuring out your home's investment value will help you to view your property realistically. You can better judge other homes as a new buyer once you understand how property values change over time.

If you have been in your home only a few years, virtually all of the profits you realize have come from increased market value. You build only a minor amount of equity by making payments on a mortgage, because those payments are largely interest in the early years. The interest is based on the outstanding balance of your loan, so you will not reduce that balance by very much during the first 5 or 10 years of a 30-year mortgage term.

With this in mind, you might find that you make little or no profit by moving. One benefit of going through the investment value analysis is discovering how much, if any, money you have really made on a strictly investment basis. If your home has appreciated in value, so have other properties that you will consider buying that are of equal or better quality.

The real value of owning a home is the collective intangibles—

security, a fixed cost of housing, control over your own property, and the gradual building of equity over many years. You can certainly continue to build equity in a new home by transferring from your present location to another one. The point is, don't make your decision to stay or move based strictly on the rate of return.

If you make a profit from the investment, it does not mean you realize it, that you "take" the money. You only transfer it to another home. And if you end up losing money on paper, you are still only transferring equity from one property to another.

Use investment value as a way to compare trends in one neighborhood over another. For instance, Eric and Sylvia Townsend decided to look for a new home. They had owned their original house for 10 years, but now wanted a larger place. They went through the investment value computation. They used it in the following way: When looking at homes in which they were interested, they asked, "What was the approximate market value of this house 10 years ago?"

The purpose was to judge how that house had appreciated in value, compared to their original house. By comparing the investment value of their own property against prospective new homes, they could determine how well the house and the neighborhood fared during the same period.

This is a valuable comparison. For example, what if you find a house that seems ideal, but the rate of return over the last decade is much lower than it was on your house? This could indicate that buying houses in that area is not as wise an investment as it was for you to buy your original house.

What is going on in that neighborhood? Are there a lot of homes for sale? How long has the house been on the market? Is there a negative transition in progress? What about crime and arson fire statistics?

Having a means of comparison makes you more aware as both a seller and a buyer, and helps your evaluation of other homes and areas. Sellers cannot operate in isolation. They must be aware of conditions in their own area *and* in the area they are considering for their new residence.

YOUR EVALUATION CHECKLIST

You should certainly research and investigate as a buyer. But also expect buyers of your home to look for flaws and make the same comparisons.

Prepare to show your home with a clear understanding of the relationship between selling your home and buying another. Take steps now, before you put your home on the market, to anticipate problems and correct them—before buyers start making offers below your asked price.

Make up a checklist of the good points and the bad points in your home (Figure 3–2). Also write down the actions you can take today to correct any problems. Cover the following areas:

1. Location of your home.
2. General condition of the property.
3. The neighborhood.

FIGURE 3–2

seller's evaluation checklist		
GOOD POINTS	BAD POINTS	ACTIONS
location:		
condition:		
neighborhood:		
market value:		
other:		

4. Market value.
5. Other important points.

Take all corrective actions in your control now, and your home will be more attractive to buyers. They might still find fault with your property, but that is to be expected. You cannot anticipate every possible flaw that someone else will notice.

Be prepared, too, for buyers who do not appreciate corrective actions you take. For instance, you might argue that you recently replaced the roof, put in new drapes and carpets, painted inside and out, did a lot of landscaping, remodeled the kitchen, and built a deck in the backyard. The problem, though, is that a buyer expects to get a house with all of these features. The buyer did not see the condition of your home before repairs and will not be more inclined to buy just because you put your house in marketable order. Don't expect your house to be *more* attractive to a stranger than it was in its previous condition. It should be enough that it is impressive in comparison with other properties the same buyer will view.

Chapter 4 explains how statistics on recent sales will help you judge the condition of the market, and help you succeed in selling your home at a fair price.

CHAPTER 4

UNDERSTANDING THE MARKET

All of the economic realities that affect your home's market value today—supply and demand, conditions in your neighborhood, crime levels, employment, and the broad perception of real estate values—can be summarized in one trend: prices of recently sold homes.

This statement must be qualified. The study of recent sales prices is, on the surface, a straightforward one. But to complete your study accurately, you must be sure to use and interpret information correctly.

THE MEANING OF SALES STATISTICS

You can easily find out the prices of homes that sold during the last two years in your neighborhood. This information is part of the public record. Your banker, real estate brokers, and other financial professionals in your area also have it. You can find the information you need by borrowing and studying the publication that lists recent sales.

To make a valid comparison, remember:

1. You must compare homes similar to yours in terms of the number of rooms, total living space, and lot size.

2. The homes must be in the same area or in neighborhoods close by that share common characteristics. Be aware that the separation of a few blocks can often mean tens of thousands of dollars difference in sale prices.

3. The prices of homes recently sold is only a part of the study. You must also look at the number of months a property was on the market before it sold, and the "swing" percentage between asked price and sales price. Finally, you must attempt to identify the way a trend is moving.

It helps to look at sales over the past year or two, but pay close attention to more recent statistics. Today's conditions ultimately will determine what your home is worth. The emphasis on these recent sales figures is valid. They reflect the perception of value among buyers. Price is largely set by supply and demand factors, and is then affected by specific conditions in your area. So the prices and length of time required to sell are critical in estimating the value of your home accurately.

EXAMPLE:

You are thinking of selling your home, so you ask your banker to lend you the report listing recent sales information. In it, you find the asked and actual sales price, date each home was placed on the market, and date of sale. Another useful piece of information is whether or not a particular home has been offered for sale in the past, with the offer withdrawn for lack of interest or suitable offers.

If you find some homes were offered and then withdrawn, it might be that they are problem properties. They might have structural problems, or perhaps title to the property is uncertain or under dispute, making it difficult or even impossible to convey ownership. If they are exceptions to the rule, exclude these homes from your averages.

You might, however, discover a large number of homes were offered for sale in the past and then withdrawn. If this is widespread, it's a sign that sellers are having great difficulty in finding suitable buyers, or that buyers think values are much lower than prevailing asked prices. In either event, it's useful information as you attempt to judge today's market conditions.

PRICE AND TIME

After eliminating unusual situations found in recent sales (such as homes that were offered and then withdrawn), you will have a good sampling of trends in your area. Next, you should identify three key factors: the swing, months on the market, and the trend.

The Swing

This is the percentage difference between the original asked price and the final sales price. To compute it, subtract one from the other, then divide the difference by the sales price.

The percentage indicates whether or not houses in your area are in demand. A high percentage shows that offers were made substantially below asked prices, and were accepted—an indication that houses are either priced too high or that buyers know an excess of properties are on the market. A lower percentage indicates the opposite—that a large number of buyers need and want housing, and are willing to pay close to the asked price.

The swing varies by area. But as a general rule, if the percentage is at or below 5 percent, it is a good sign for sellers. It indicates houses are selling close to asked prices.

Months on the Market

The length of time it takes to actually close a deal is also revealing. When demand is high, houses sell within the first month. If houses in your area are selling in three months or less, that is considered a highly favorable level of demand, a good sign for sellers. If the average is between four and six months, that is generally acceptable. But if the time is six months or more, then sellers face a tough battle attracting buyers.

The Trend

Like all statistics, averages can be deceiving. It is not so much the level over a period of months that counts, but the direction of the trend. For instance, if the swing in your area averages 7 percent that tells you very little by itself. But if that average was 10 percent one year ago, the trend is taking a favorable direction.

The same applies to time on the market. The overall average might be four months, but the most recent sales might have closed in two months or less.

Look at the asked price, sales price, swing, and months on the market for the last two years. Then compute the averages in six-month segments. This will reveal how current conditions favor either sellers or buyers. If you find that the trend is toward lower swing percentages and a shorter time on the market, you should also expect to see an increase in average prices of houses similar to yours. The swing and length of time to sell point to increasing demand.

DOING THE STUDY

To compile the information needed to judge the market, take these steps:

1. Identify homes listed in the report that are in your area and are similar in terms of number of rooms and approximate size.

2. List the asked price, sales price, and number of months on the market. But exclude any exceptional cases that might distort your averages.

Make a chart listing the information in these first two steps like the one shown in Figure 4–1.

3. Compute the average asked price. Add the total of all asked prices, and then divide the total by the number of properties involved.
4. Compute the average sales price. Add the total of all sales prices, and then divide the total by the number of homes sold.
5. Figure out the swing. Subtract average sales price from average asked price; then divide the balance by the average sales price. (Swing can also be computed by basing it on percentage of asked price, or by simply dividing one average price from the other. You can use any of these methods, as long as you develop a consistent method for making your comparison.)
6. Figure out the average number of months homes were on the market. Add the total months, and then divide by the number of properties.

A summary of these steps is shown in Figure 4–2.

Remember that the overall average is informative, but the most recent averages are the most relevant to you. Compare the overall picture to statistics for only the last six months.

FIGURE 4–1
Recent Sales Statistics

ASKED PRICE	SALE PRICE	MONTHS ON THE MARKET
$101,950	$ 95,000	2
96,500	94,500	2
98,000	98,000	4
103,500	95,000	4
99,500	91,500	5
106,750	101,750	7

FIGURE 4–2
The Swing

average asked price	$101,033
average sale price	$ 95,958
swing	5.3%
average time on the market	4 months

INTERPRETING YOUR RESULTS

How do you convert what you discover from this study into an estimation of what you can expect to receive upon sale of your home? Most sellers depend on the advice of real estate brokers and their appraisers to recommend a price. As an informed seller, you should gather all the information possible before putting your home on the market. This study is an important step as you begin to think like a seller. It's your property, and you should be armed with adequate information.

Assume the swing is on the increase. Over the last two years, the average has been 6 percent. But in the most recent six months, it has been 8 percent. This is a sign that buyers perceive homes like yours as being overpriced. If the trend is toward lower sales prices, you must be willing to anticipate that trend and price your home accordingly. If, however, you are in no particular hurry, ask a higher price and decide what offer you would actually accept.

If the swing is more favorable, you have an advantage. What if the two-year average is 6 percent, but the most recent figures show only a 4 percent swing? In this case, you should expect to get offers close to the price you advertise.

You will probably also notice that the average sales prices of homes have been moving upward with the trend in swing. As a rule, as the swing declines (a sign of increased buyer demand), prices will rise. But because you are studying *recent* statistics, this growth in demand might be too subtle for many sellers to recognize. Understanding the swing gives you the advantage. Even if the price you insist on is higher than the price a real estate broker recommends, you might still get an attractive offer.

MARKET CONDITIONS

Certain conditions in your area could affect the actual fair market value of your property, in spite of recent sales figures. The following examples illustrate some of these conditions.

1. A large company lays off a number of its employees. Hundreds of people decide to move at the same time, creating at least a temporary distortion in supply and demand. A new employer might also come into the area, creating a sudden demand for workers and, with it, an unexpected rise in the demand for housing.

2. Interest rates can rise or fall in a relatively short period of time. Current rates have a direct impact on housing values; in some conditions, the effect outweighs all other considerations. When rates are extremely high, a sale might be made or broken based on the buyer's ability to obtain attractive financing.

3. Your community might place a moratorium on construction, or indirectly impede building in other ways, by limiting new water hookups, for example. Conversely, a long-standing moratorium could be lifted. Either of these situations could change the climate of supply and demand very suddenly.

The economic conditions, interest rates, and regulatory restrictions in your area all affect the type of market you will face as a seller. These points, along with the natural supply and demand for housing, will all affect the price you get.

Your preliminary study of sales statistics should tell you whether you are now in a buyer's or a seller's market. A high swing between asked and sales prices and an increasing number of months required to sell homes are the signs of a buyer's market. There are more properties available and fewer buyers. So each buyer has the luxury of comparing a large number of homes and time to look for the best deal. (See Figure 4–3.)

A low swing and shorter number of months homes are on the market point to a seller's market. In this case, the average sales price should also

FIGURE 4–3
Buyer's Market

be on the rise. A larger number of buyers are seeking homes, but there are not enough homes to go around. Because of this, prices rise and it takes less time to sell. (See Figure 4–4.)

SPOTTING A TREND

Trends rather than an isolated month's condition will indicate whether you are in a buyer's or a seller's market. Look for the signs.

A simple comparison of the number of homes available each month, to the number sold, will be quite revealing. This comparison should be on an average basis, because month-to-month availability and sales do not refer to the sale properties. For example, if 16 homes go on the market in one month, and 9 sell, that by itself doesn't tell you how quickly the 16 homes will move. You don't know what will happen in the immediate future, nor what took place in the months preceding.

Figure 4–5 shows how availability versus actual sales can be compared. This information can be found in the same report your banker or real estate broker receives each month. The buyer's market shows that

FIGURE 4–4
Seller's Market

FIGURE 4–5

trends in market demand

buyer's market   seller's market

MONTH	HOMES FOR SALE	SALES
Jan	16	9
Feb	12	6
Mar	15	8
Apr	15	5
May	17	7
Jun	14	6

MONTH	HOMES FOR SALE	SALES
Jan	10	10
Feb	9	8
Mar	11	9
Apr	8	8
May	8	6
Jun	6	5

only a portion of available homes sell each month, on average. Thus, a large inventory of properties is offered, but demand lags behind. The seller's market, however, shows that availability and actual sales are closely matched. Homes are being sold over the six-month period. Obviously, demand is high and may even be greater than the supply.

There is no simple way to evaluate the market and current conditions to make absolute conclusions. You can only gather and consolidate information from as many sources as possible. Your preliminary study of swing and time should be added to the advice of a real estate broker, and judged in the context of an appraiser's opinion. In the following chapter, how an appraiser views your home, what methods are used to estimate value, and what that means to you are discussed.

CHAPTER 5

GETTING AN APPRAISAL

An appraisal is strictly an estimate of your home's current market value. No one can define exactly what any home is worth, so the most scientific and reasonable methods must be used to establish the estimate.

The *real* value of your home is the agreed upon price that you, the seller, and a buyer determine. *Market* value should be defined as the lowest price you are willing to accept, and the highest price a buyer is willing to pay. Obviously, many factors will affect this price. The availability of similar homes and the prices they are offered for, the number of buyers, interest rates, quality, location, condition, extras, and improvements—all of these as well as other points all alter the actual market value of your home.

THE INDEPENDENT APPRAISER

Most appraisals take place from the seller's point of view in an informal manner. Real estate brokers will individually assess a property's value based on their working knowledge of the market and all current conditions. They see many similar homes in the course of their work, and usually have the best instincts about the price you can expect to get.

For a buyer to qualify for financing, a lender usually calls for an appraisal, either by an independent person or company, or by one of their own employees. Chances are, the value you assign to your home will differ from the appraisal value a lender ends up with. Understanding that the bank, savings and loan, or other institution will be taking a risk by providing financing to the buyer, expect their appraisal value to be conservative in comparison to the maximum market value you and your broker would like to get.

Many lenders appraise properties using their own loan officers. These people might understand market value and risk quite well, but sometimes have no formal training as appraisers. Their estimates are based on experience in granting loans to buyers. In fact, there is no uniform standard, license, or degree that qualifies an individual to conduct an appraisal. Unlike the certification and required licensing of physicians, attorneys, and accountants in every state, appraisals can be practiced by anyone.

An *independent* appraisal is one conducted by an individual with no vested interest in the determination of market value. Certainly, a bank or savings institution has vested interest if mortgage money will be loaned on the basis of an appraisal. Most states do not impose any regulatory standards on individuals offering appraisal services. However, to ensure that an individual has had some training and experience and knows how to conduct a professional appraisal, contact one of these two national organizations:

1. The American Institute of Real Estate Appraisers (AIREA) tests its members and grants appraisal licenses to those with proven qualifications and experience. The MAI (Member, Appraisal Institute) and the RM (Residential Member) are both tested and qualified. For more information or a list of local professionals, write to AIREA at 430 North Michigan Avenue, Chicago IL 60611 (312–329–8559).

2. The Society of Real Estate Appraisers also tests members and grants licenses to those qualified and experienced to offer professional services. The SRA (Senior Residential Appraiser) and SREA (Senior Real Estate Analyst) are both qualified to offer professional appraisal services. For further information or a list of local members, write to The Society at 645 North Michigan Avenue, Chicago IL 60611 (800–331–7732; 312–346–7422 in Illinois).

THE MARKET COMPARISON APPROACH

When would you, as a seller, want an appraisal? As a general rule, you will place your home on the market if you agree with the broker's suggested asked price, and if you are willing to accept a reasonable offer from a buyer. But if a potential lender's opinion of value is so much lower than yours that buyers cannot qualify for financing, an independent opinion might become necessary.

In this case, an independent appraisal can be sought by the seller. For a cost ranging between $200 and $350, a professional affiliated with one of the two organizations just mentioned will provide you with a written appraisal of your home.

Appraisers use several methods to value residential property. The most common of these is the market comparison approach. You are already familiar with this technique, described in Chapter 4. The appraisal is based on recent sale prices of similar homes in the same area. The formal market comparison approach an appraiser would use includes adjustments to arrive at a fair market value. The process includes allowances for:

1. Recent sales prices.
2. Adjustments for special features, such as extra rooms, unusually large lot size, actual square feet of living space above or below the average home, condition of your property, a better-than-average view.
3. Dates of recent sales, because economic conditions (supply and demand, interest rates, employment statistics) might have changed in the very recent past.
4. Terms of the sale, including interest rates, the amount to be financed, and how much, if any, of the balance you will carry as a second mortgage.
5. Location. For example, the average sale in your area might be on relatively quiet residential streets, whereas your house fronts on a busy main thoroughfare. The noise factor will reduce the market value of your home.

The range of recent sales prices, adjusted for any current economic trends, is adjusted upward or downward for special features and conditions to arrive at the estimated market value. This is shown in Figure 5–1.

FIGURE 5–1
Market Comparison Approach

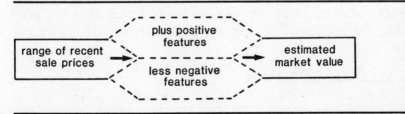

THE COST APPROACH

A thorough appraisal might be based entirely on the market comparison approach, or it might combine several appraisal methods.

EXAMPLE:

Your home is being put on the market. But in your area, the frequency of home sales is quite low. Thus, in the appraiser's opinion, there is not a large enough sampling to accurately appraise your home on the basis of market comparison alone.

In this case, the appraiser could use the cost approach. With this appraisal method, the value of the land is first estimated. This is based on the estimated value your lot would have if no home existed. The reasonable market value is then developed based on prices of vacant residential lots in your area.

The cost to construct a home on the lot at today's prices is then added to the land value. A final adjustment is made for depreciation. Based on the age and general condition of your home, an amount is taken off the estimate for wear and tear, deterioration, and system obsolescence (for example, the plumbing, electrical wiring, or heating system might be out of date by today's standards). The net result of these estimates is the appraised value of your home under the cost approach.

There are two methods for estimating the cost of construction. First is reproduction cost, the amount required to create an exact duplicate. If your home includes built-in, hand-carved banisters and bookshelves, hardwood floors, and custom features not standard under today's construction standards, then reproduction cost will be higher than the average cost of construction.

A second way to estimate construction cost is the replacement cost method. This is an estimate of the cost to build a home that is functionally the same as yours, but not an exact duplicate.

In actual practice, the cost approach is rarely used for residential housing. It is more appropriate for properties that are not bought and sold regularly, such as special-purpose structures (churches, government buildings, and museums). The cost approach is summarized in Figure 5–2.

THE INCOME APPROACH

A third method, the income approach, is used for homes that are rented out as income property. The appraisal is based on the theory that future

FIGURE 5–2
Cost Approach

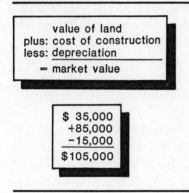

```
        value of land
plus: cost of construction
less: depreciation
  = market value
```

```
$ 35,000
+85,000
-15,000
$105,000
```

market value will be determined by the potential for generating profits to an investor.

EXAMPLE:

You are selling a second home that has been rented out for the last few years. The appraiser decides to combine the market comparison and income approaches in determining estimated market value.

To figure value under the income approach, the annual gross income is computed, then reduced for a reasonable estimate of vacancies (including the possibility of uncollected rents in an occupied house). For instance, you receive approximately $19,000 when your home is rented all year round. But the appraiser deducts 15 percent, or $2,850, for vacancies and the possibility of unpaid rents.

From this number, operating expenses are deducted. These include insurance, maintenance, property taxes, and other costs related to the income property. When the operating expenses are deducted, the estimated net annual income remains.

EXAMPLE:

In your case, operating expenses add up to $3,650 on average. Taking the gross of $19,000 and deducting the 15 percent for vacancies and operating expenses, estimated annual net income is $12,500.

Next, a capitalization rate is applied to the net income. This is where the biggest problem comes in. The "cap" rate is a rough estimate based on similar income properties. It can vary, though, because other properties may be located in slightly better or worse areas, demand can vary, and another individual will have better or worse experiences with tenants. Appraisers might apply an average capitalization rate based on several similar properties, in an attempt to arrive at a fair average.

The cap rate is figured by dividing net income from other properties, by the sales price. For example, one home recently sold for $149,500. Its annual net income averaged $12,300. The cap rate is 8.2 percent ($12,300 divided by $149,500).

To estimate the market value of your rental house, your average net income is divided by the cap rate. If you have averaged $12,500 in net income, using the 8.2 percent average, your home's market value will be estimated at $152,439 ($12,500 divided by 8.2 percent). The computation is summarized in Figure 5–3.

FIGURE 5–3
Income Approach

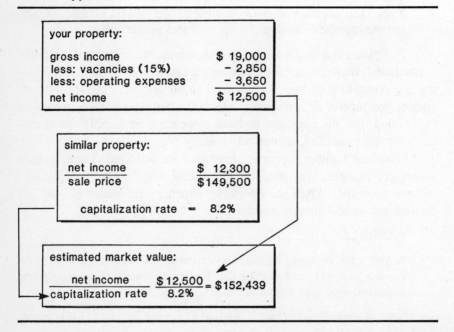

APPRAISAL OPINIONS

Everyone will have a different opinion of your home's value. The buyer, in many circumstances, will offer less than you want. The real estate broker might want to price the home to sell quickly, or might want to get maximum dollar (depending on the general conditions of the market and competition for sales). The lender will appraise your property most conservatively of all. The policies will be restrictive, in order to minimize risks. One lender might advance up to 80 percent of the appraised value, and the buyer has to come up with the difference. Raising 20 percent is difficult enough. If there is also a big gap between the asked price and the lender's appraised value, you might need an independent opinion to convince the lender that its own appraisal is overly conservative.

Reconciling appraised value with the price you want is made all the more difficult if your house has inherent problems. If, for example, its design, age, or the neighborhood itself are undesirable to buyers, you will have to deal with these factors when you put your home on the market. The next chapter explores such problems.

CHAPTER 6

IF YOU HAVE
A PROBLEM HOUSE

Some houses are especially difficult to sell. In comparison with other properties on the market, certain features or conditions of your property may reduce its value. The four major problems concern design, energy efficiency, behind-the-wall systems, and the neighborhood.

When buyers look at the houses on the market, they are shopping by comparison. So an older, poorly maintained, or poorly designed house will not be as appealing as a newer one. This is the case even when construction quality is better in the older property, or when asked price is a better bargain. You might price your home to sell quickly, only to discover that buyers want newer, more cheaply built homes that command thousands of dollars more in price. The analysis of recent sales prices, the level of supply and demand, and advantages of location, can all become meaningless if your house simply will not sell. These problems can be reduced or even eliminated, though, with a little planning.

DESIGN PROBLEMS

Real estate brokers will tell you that most buyers decide very quickly whether or not they "like" a house. If their first impression is negative, it is usually formed as soon as they see the house. A buyer enters through your front door and looks around. If the view is not a pleasing one, chances are that no offer will come from that buyer, even if the price, size, location, and financing are all just right. Even though a home is the largest investment most of us make, we tend to base our decisions on immediate impressions rather than on thorough investigation.

The design problems in your house might be easily solved. A smart buyer, recognizing this, will make an offer, buy the house, and invest a few thousand dollars to make the necessary changes. You can do the same thing before showing your home, and realize a profit in a higher sales price.

By today's standards, a design "problem" might be a simple matter of taste and style. The idea that a home's space should be planned is relatively new. After World War II, when the United States suffered a severe housing shortage, tract homes were built as quickly as possible. The question of planning the interior never came up. Builders simply wanted to build functional homes as quickly as possible.

Many of these homes are laid out in a rectangle or L-shape, and offer just the basics: a living room, dining area, kitchen, three bedrooms, a bath, and a garage. The design is simple. But today's buyer might view the basic tract layout negatively for a number of reasons.

The floor plan shown in Figure 6–1 is a typical tract design. A buyer might view this property not just in terms of price, location, and condition, but as a house with an unimaginative and limited design. The design problems here can be solved with a few changes. As a seller, your investment in these changes will be more than justified. Chances are, you will receive offers more promptly and at amounts closer to your asked price by investing a few thousand dollars.

The design problems are as follows:

1. *The front door opens directly into the living room.* Whenever people come to the door, they will immediately see this area. Because every other part of the house also connects to this main room, it will suffer a lot of traffic. There is no sense of privacy or intimacy.

2. *The kitchen is also open and visible from the living room.* The lack of separation is an inconvenience to those in the living room, especially while a meal is being prepared.

3. *The house has only one bathroom.* Newer homes will invariably have two or more baths, and the limitation in this floor plan will reduce the value of the home considerably.

4. *Access to the backyard can be made only through the kitchen.* This means a lot of traffic, an inconvenience that may buyers will not want to tolerate.

These four design problems can be easily solved. First, the area of the living room between the kitchen entrance and the front door is virtually wasted. Because people use this to get from one area of the house to another, it is a high-traffic section of the house. Thus, you will not lose anything by reducing the open space. Suggested solutions:

1. *Build a small entranceway, including a front closet.* It will block the view from the living room, affording a desirable level of privacy; it also adds a closet, giving guests a convenient place to hang their coats. A

FIGURE 6–1
Design Problems

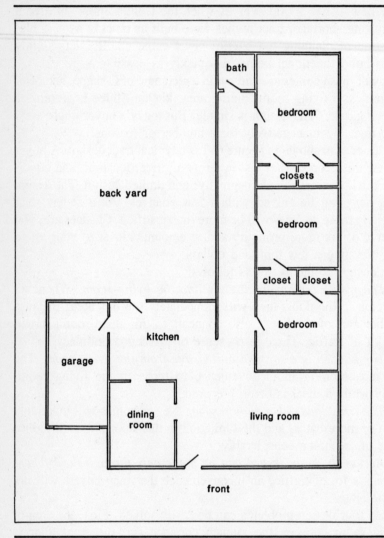

well-lighted entrance, plus pictures on the walls, will improve the first impression made on buyers.

2. *Extend the kitchen hallway wall forward a few feet, and add a swinging door between the kitchen and the living room.* This will block the view from the living room, reduce noise and smoke, and create a more desirable atmosphere.

FIGURE 6–2
Design Improvements

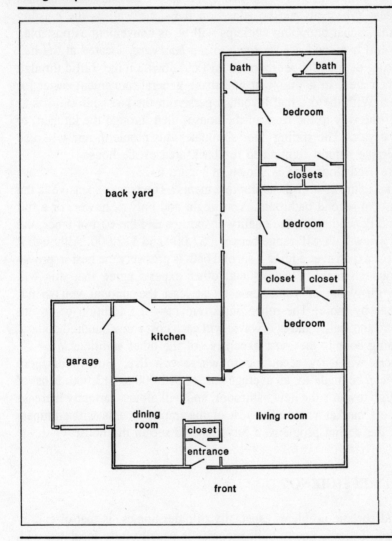

front

3. *Add a door between the living room and the hallway,* so that the living room can be closed off from the rest of the house. This door can be left open most of the time, but closed if some people are trying to sleep, while others are still up. The door also makes it easier to heat and cool sections of the house. By closing off areas, greater efficiency is achieved.

4. *Add a second bath in the largest bedroom,* the last one down the hall. This room is probably the master bedroom, as it already contains two closets. The bath can be added on the same wall as the existing bathroom, so that plumbing hookups will be as convenient as possible.

5. *Add a second access route to the backyard,* located at the hall across from the middle bedroom. It will cut down on the traffic through the kitchen area. In addition, it will make general movement easier for everyone. With the original layout, a person in the last bedroom has to travel all the way to the front of the house, then through the kitchen, to get to the yard. The sliding door eliminates this problem, and will also add desirable natural lighting to the back area of the house.

A revised floor plan is shown in Figure 6–2.

What is the cost of these improvements? The most expensive is the addition of a second bathroom. You might add only a shower, or a full bath. And depending on the quality of fixtures and the cost of labor, the price of a new bath will range between $7,000 and $12,000. Although it is the most expensive, adding a second bath is probably the best improvement you can make. Realtors and other experts agree that this will increase the value of your home by at least the amount you spend, sometimes by more. The other improvements—the addition of an entranceway and walls, and doorways, will each cost a few hundred dollars. The sliding door is the most expensive of the other additions.

Prices will vary according to where you live. But all of these changes can be made for an average cost of $10,000 to $13,000. Most of this will go towards the new bathroom, and will almost certainly increase the home's market value. The rest of the improvements will eliminate most of the design problems a buyer would see in the house.

ENERGY EFFICIENCY

A second chronic problem, especially in older homes, is that of energy efficiency. Today's newly built property is usually fully insulated with windows that resist the cold. Energy conservation was not a great concern before the 1970s, so if your home was built before that decade, it probably has energy problems. Some solutions:

1. *Put weather stripping on all windows and doors.* You need only a hammer, a screwdriver, and the materials you can buy at any hardware store.

For doors, buy a threshold and door-sweep combination. Use rain-drip weather strip on garage doors and other doors with bottom gaps. To reduce drafts at the edge of doors, use spring or cushion metal ribbons.

For louver windows, use clear weather strip that can be cut and snapped or glued onto the end of louvers. For inside doors, use bottom sweeps or automatic door bottoms. For odd-shaped areas, buy a roll of self-adhesive strip made of polyurethane, neoprene, or vinyl foam.

2. *Insulate attics.* This will save up to one fourth of the total heating costs in most areas of the country. The insulation that is easiest to install is mineral wool, available in blankets or 4-by-8-foot batts. You can also insulate with pouring wool, cellulose, foam, or expanding materials like vermiculite or perlite.

The degree of attic insulation will vary depending on the extremes of cold and heat in your area. The R-value (resistance level to heat and cold) is measured numerically. In warmer areas, R-19 is recommended as a minimum; higher R-values of R-30 or more, should be installed in colder climates.

The R-value varies with the type of insulation you install. An approximate guideline:

Inches	Blown-in fiberglass	Blown-in mineral wool	Fiberglass batts	Blown-in cellulose
14				
13	R-30			
12				
11				
10	R-24	R-30		
9	R-19	R-24	R-30	
8			R-24	R-30
7		R-19	R-19	R-24
6	R-11			
5				R-19
4		R-11	R-11	
3				R-11
2				
1				

3. *Insulate existing walls,* using cellulose, foam, or mineral wool. You should hire a contractor to properly insulate with these materials.

4. *Insulate floors,* using blankets or batts. Also add insulation to heating ducts, using mineral wool duct wrap, and cover your hot-water heater with an insulation blanket.

5. *Replace old or cracked windows* with double-pane plastic or glass storm windows. This will reduce window heat loss by 50 percent in many regions.

6. *Install heat-reflecting glass, awnings, or window screens* to reduce heat during summer months.

You can take care of most energy-savings steps on your own, without having to hire an expert. Before you begin, however, check with your local gas and electric company. Most public utilities have free literature with ideas for making your home energy-efficient.

Some precautions when working with insulation are:

1. Always wear a face mask when installing machine-blown insulation.
2. If you are not sure about safety or the right method for installing insulation, hire a contractor.
3. Always wear gloves and a long-sleeve shirt to avoid irritation from insulation fibers.
4. Do not smoke in attics and other confined areas when installing insulation.
5. Don't insulate over the top of recessed light fixtures, chimneys, or flues. Keep insulation at least 3 inches away from all heat-producing equipment. Cut the ends off a tin can and place the can around the heat producing equipment before installing insulation.
6. Do not cover eave vents, closet vents, or heating and cooling equipment vents with insulation.

PLUMBING AND ELECTRICAL SYSTEMS

One reason buyers often want new rather than old homes is fear of what cannot be seen. The condition of behind-the-wall systems for plumbing and electrical wiring is not visible, and the older the home, the greater the chance of expensive repair problems in the near future.

You must expect to pay for a complete house inspection (see Chapter 7) when you place your home on the market. A professional inspector will evaluate the condition of behind-the-wall systems and point out any problems you have. But before taking that step, you can eliminate some of the more obvious problems on your own.

Your electrical system should be set up to handle 220-volt wiring. Many older homes were not designed with enough power to handle air conditioning, electrical heating systems, and electric washers and dryers.

If your system does not have 220-volt wiring, hire an electrical contractor and have it installed.

Your fuse box should be set up with no less than 100 amps if the system must service a dishwasher, air conditioner, and other power-draining equipment. If your fuse box has less than this minimum, plan to hire an electrician to upgrade it. And replace a fuse system with circuit breakers.

Check with your local building inspector for today's minimum requirements for electrical systems. In some areas, homes put up for sale must be brought up to a minimum standard. And many older homes don't meet those standards. You might be required to install additional electrical outlets, to ground your entire electrical system, or take other steps to either increase power or reduce danger.

If your water supply comes from a well on your property, questions of pressure, storage tank capacity, and condition of your pump should be raised and answered. A home inspection will address these concerns.

The major question regarding plumbing is the type and condition of pipes. Older plumbing systems might have been built of galvanized iron. Mineral deposits accumulate in iron pipes over time, affecting the water flow. Brass or copper pipes are preferable, and today, copper or plastic piping is often used. You can identify galvanized iron pipes by attaching a magnet. If the magnet is attracted to the pipe, it is iron. You cannot tell what type of pipes you have just by their color.

Check for leaks by looking for water stains around exposed piping. Carefully check joints connecting one length of pipe to another. This is a likely place for leaks to develop.

Make any repairs you discover are needed. However, you might want to wait until a home inspector completes an evaluation, so that *all* necessary maintenance can be performed at the same time. An extremely worn plumbing system might have to be replaced in part, which is expensive and requires hiring a professional contractor. But not upgrading these problems might lead to a buyer negotiating your price down because plumbing is not up-to-date nor constructed of the most durable materials. Even worse, buyers might simply bypass your home entirely.

THE NEIGHBORHOOD

You have the opportunity to upgrade your house for design problems, energy efficiency, and electrical or plumbing systems. But when it comes to the overall condition of your neighborhood, there is much less you can do to create a positive impression.

The general range of prices for homes similar to yours will be determined to a great extent by the condition of the neighborhood. A well-maintained, strictly residential area will command higher prices than a run-down area with both residential and commercial properties, traffic noise, empty houses, vacant lots, high incidence of crime, and unmanicured front lawns.

Start by making sure your home creates a positive impression. Mow the lawn, trim the hedges, and paint the exterior if needed. No roof tiles should be missing, and visible foundation areas should be free of open cracks. Paint fences, paint or pave over oil stains in your driveway, and repair loose stones on walls. In other words, take the steps needed to show you home at its best.

The neighborhood itself is beyond your immediate control. But you should be aware of its condition before placing your home on the market, so that you will know what to expect from buyers. Drive around your area and judge its conditions:

Positive	*Negative*
Many homes are undergoing improvements—new rooms are being added, properties are being upgraded.	Many homes are for sale or left vacant. Some lots are empty and no building is taking place.
Homes are painted and in good repair.	Repairs are not made even on the exteriors.
Lawns are kept mowed, hedges trimmed.	Front yards are overgrown with weeds.
Few homes are for sale, and most are occupied by the owners.	Many homes are for sale, stay on the market for months, and are rented out.
The area is strictly a residential one.	Service stations and fast-food restaurants are mixed in with housing.
Traffic noise is minimal, and congestion is not a problem.	Traffic is congested and noisy.

Most buyers are not thorough enough in checking these points. But if a buyer does ask questions, you must be prepared to: (1) have the answers to those questions, and (2) accept a lower sale price for your home if conditions are so negative that your home will not sell otherwise.

PRICING THE PROBLEM HOUSE

Sellers are often disappointed to discover that a potential buyer is not willing to pay more for a home after several thousands of dollars have been spent on repairs. For instance, you might fix up your front yard, paint inside and out, put on a new roof, and insulate all around. But the buyer still offers a price that's only about the same as other homes in the area. You must recognize the realities about repairs made in anticipation of a sale:

1. The buyer *expects* the property to be in the best possible condition, and will not be willing to pay for getting the property in shape.
2. The buyer did not see the "before," only the "after." While you might see a tremendous difference in condition and appearance, the buyer cannot appreciate all that you have done.
3. If repairs simply bring the house up to acceptable standards, that's a cost you must be willing to bear.
4. Some expenses must be undertaken to conform to the current building code. For example, in some areas, homeowners are required to install smoke alarms in any house put on the market. You cannot expect the buyer to pay for these extras.
5. If your neighborhood is not the most desirable place to live, the value of your improvements will be limited. Buyers will not be willing to exceed a maximum perceived value for a house in your area.

Some problems can be solved with an investment of time and money. Other conditions, such as a declining neighborhood, cannot be fixed by you personally when you put your home on the market. In setting a price for your home, you can take one of two possible approaches. First, you can lower the price, based on what you discover about the area and other values. This will make your property more competitive than a similar home that is priced higher. Second, you can place a higher asked price on your home, but be willing to accept a lower offer.

The next chapter explains your legal obligations, along with guidelines for selecting a professional home inspector.

CHAPTER 7

LEGAL OBLIGATIONS OF SELLERS

You're about to put your house on the market, but you discover that the foundation must be replaced. Or you have $8,000 in termite damage. Or your roof leaks in four places. Can you apply the principle of *caveat emptor* (let the buyer beware)?

No, you cannot. In the past, once the papers were signed, the buyer was on his own. If he didn't discover any damage before buying your house, that was not your problem. But beginning in 1984, courts in several states set precedents in this area. They concluded that sellers and their agents are required to tell buyers about defects.

BROKER AND SELLER LIABILITY

A real estate broker's responsibilities are given in detail in Chapter 12. For now, it is simply important to understand that when a broker represents you as the seller, you share in the responsibility to disclose faults in your property. The broker's liability (and yours, too) could be significant. In one case, a California State Court of Appeals issued a statement as part of its decision that imposed on the broker "an affirmative duty to conduct a reasonably competent and diligent inspection of the residential property listed for sale and to disclose to prospective purchasers all facts materially affecting the value or desirability of the property that such an investigation would reveal."[1]

This decision and similar rulings in other states place the seller and the broker in a new position. Not only must you disclose all *known* facts to a buyer; you must also investigate and search for any defects that a "diligent inspection" would reveal.

---

[1]*Easton v. Strassburger*, A010566, California First District Court of Appeal (February, 1984).

What does this mean? Should the broker, by virtue of professional experience, be able to examine a house inside and out, and find any and all defects? Probably not. Virtually all homes must be inspected professionally before they are sold. The inspection—performed by an independent contractor or other professional—is thought to satisfy the requirement for a "reasonably competent and diligent inspection." To a degree, it does protect you and your real estate agent from future lawsuits.

As a result of this new direction in court rulings, real estate brokers are now more likely to insist on a complete home inspection, as part of the process of putting your home on the market. Certainly, a litigious buyer could still sue you, the broker, and perhaps the home inspector, even several years after the sale was completed. But having conducted the inspection will defuse the strongest possible argument—that you should have known about a defect, and should have disclosed it to the buyer.

Buyers who discover defects in previously purchased homes will continue to file lawsuits. But because brokers are now calling for diligent independent inspections, the home inspector is often named as a defendant, along with the seller and the broker.

Your best protection against future claims for flaws discovered after you sell your property is a thorough evaluation, with a written report for the buyer. As long as everyone—the seller, the broker, and the inspector—does their part in discovering and disclosing any flaws, the chances of a future claim are reduced.

THE COMPLETE INSPECTION

A thorough inspection should include an examination of every part of your house, from the basement or cellar to the roof, inside and outside components and additions, and all appliances and systems. Most sellers are already aware of the need for a termite inspection. But that is usually separate from the home inspection. Many states ban home inspectors from even mentioning termite or other infestation problems in their reports. Only a licensed termite inspector can deal with those problems.

The home inspection should include an examination of 10 major areas:

1. *Foundation and basement:* defects or faults; leakage or flooding.

2. *Plumbing:* worn or leaking pipes; water pressure; water heater.
3. *Electrical:* amperage; wiring; grounding; outlets.
4. *Exterior conditions:* masonry; siding; fences and walls; sills; garage or carport.
5. *Grounds:* lawn and shrubs; driveway and walkways; steps and porches; drainage.
6. *Roof:* type and age; gutters and downspouts; chimney lining and flow; masonry.
7. *Heating and cooling:* furnace; fire hazards; efficiency; insulation.
8. *Appliances:* age; efficiency.
9. *Interior conditions:* stairs; floors, ceilings, walls; quality of construction.
10. *Doors and windows:* seepage; drafts; alignment.

An inspection checklist is shown in Figure 7–1. Be sure that the inspector you hire will evaluate all of the points. These are the major areas of a complete inspection. Many other tests will also be conducted and reported by the professional who visits your home and writes a report.

FINDING A PROFESSIONAL INSPECTOR

Homeowners can obtain a home inspection whenever they want, whether or not they plan to move. A home inspection can be used as an inexpensive way to identify problems requiring preventive maintenance.

Once you become a seller, though, the inspection will become a requirement in most states. You can order one before contacting a real estate broker; or, you can wait and leave the timing up to the broker. If you call for an inspection many months before a buyer comes to you with a serious offer, the broker might insist on an updated inspection. In that case, you could end up paying for the job twice.

How do you find a qualified, professional home inspector? Many contractors will gladly inspect your home for a fee, as a way to raise business for themselves. They identify problems, and then offer to fix them. This is similar to taking your car to a mechanic who needs the work, and asking him to fix anything that needs fixing. The incentive is to find something wrong.

FIGURE 7–1
Home Inspection Checklist

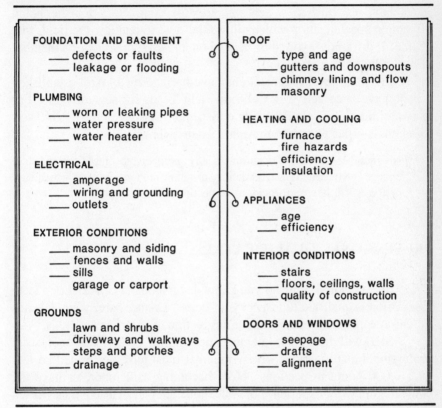

Some contractors appear to avoid this conflict of interest by offering to refer you to someone else. But that could also be a conflict. You have no way of knowing what arrangements have been made between the inspector and the contractor. If a finder's fee or some other form of compensation is paid for referrals, you will not get a completely objective inspection.

One national group sets standards for its members to resolve such problems. The American Society of Home Inspectors (ASHI), formed in 1976, sets professional standards and includes this statement in its bylaws:

> Members shall not repair any condition found during inspections and shall not endorse or recommend individuals or businesses for repair work.

The home inspection industry is relatively new, and few states impose regulatory standards as they do on contractors. A small number of states have established a new category of contractors for the home inspection specialization which allows the state to regulate the field, to a degree. But for now, you must depend on an ASHI member or a member of a similar state association.

Some state-level organizations have been formed. Well-established groups have been active in California and Texas for several years. For example, the California Real Estate Inspection Association (CREIA) sets standards similar to those of ASHI. Their bylaws state:

> No member of the Association, in any membership classification, shall engage in construction, remodeling, or repair on a property on which they or their firm has performed an inspection.

PROFESSIONAL QUALIFICATIONS

Even with standards, how do you know that a member of ASHI or a state association is qualified to inspect your home? Chances are, your state has no enforceable standard for home inspection.

ASHI will not grant membership until a person has met strict professional qualifications. Every member must have performed no less than 1,000 home inspections before becoming a member, or have the equivalent in work experience or education. They must also pass a written examination. To maintain their membership, members must also participate in a continuing education program. And at the time they join, they must perform an actual home inspection under the supervision of an ASHI representative.

While ASHI does not require its members to hold a state contractor's license, this is yet another way for you to pick the best and most qualified person to inspect your home. If you can find an inspector with ASHI membership *and* a contractor's license, you have done all that you can to ensure a professional and thorough job, one that meets the test of a "reasonably competent and diligent inspection."

The price of a home inspection varies by region and by the number of miles the individual has to travel to get to your house. As a rule, though, the fee will range between $250 and $500. Because there appears to be a growing trend to include home inspectors in lawsuits for discovered defects, these fees might become significantly higher in the near future. As the inspector's risks increase, the price of the service will also rise.

Make sure that the inspector will prepare a written report, detailing defects and their causes, for every component of your home, inside and out. A thorough buyer will insist on being given a copy of the report. And providing the report will meet the disclosure test that some courts now require as a matter of law.

Inspectors will probably include in their reports a disclaimer about any warranties or guarantees. With the threat of a lawsuit from a buyer who believes a defect was not disclosed at the time of sale, inspectors are more careful today than in the past.

You can locate a local member of ASHI by checking the telephone book, asking your real estate broker or banker for a referral, or contacting ASHI at 1010 Wisconsin Avenue, N.E., Washington DC 20007 (202–842–3096).

Figure 7–2 summarizes the qualifications you should look for in a home inspector. The first three questions should be answered yes, the last two should be answered no.

FIGURE 7–2
Qualifying a Home Inspector

DESCRIPTION	YES	NO
member of ASHI or a state association	✓	
licensed contractor	✓	
prepares a written report	✓	
will offer to perform repairs		✓
will refer others to perform repairs		✓

THE TERMITE INSPECTION

Besides having your entire home checked for defects, you must also pay for a termite inspection. When you place your home on the market, the real estate broker will call for this inspection as one of the first steps in the selling process.

Termite inspectors specialize in identifying conditions caused by a number of pests, including subterranean or drywood termites, carpenter ants, and powder-post beetles. Among these pests, subterranean termites cause the greatest amount of damage to homes in North America. Temperate regions (especially the Gulf Coast and the Southwest) are hardest hit, but homes in all states except Alaska are at risk.

The U.S. Department of Agriculture estimates that termite control costs no less than $250 million each year. This estimate does not include the cost of undetected damage, which is probably even greater than the known yearly totals.

Because damage is so extensive, a termite inspection is usually automatic. Infestation can occur so quickly that even newly constructed homes may show evidence of problems. Before you or your real estate broker call a termite inspector, you can check your own property for signs of problems.

Winged adult termites and ants are easily distinguished by several characteristics (see Figure 7–3):

Termites	*Ants*
The antenna is straight.	The antenna is elbowed.
Pairs of wings are similar in size, shape, and pattern and contain many veins.	Pairs of wings are not the same size, and have few veins.
Stubs remain when wings are detached.	Detached wings leave no stubs.
Middle part of body is thick.	Middle part of body is very narrow.

You can identify signs of termite presence even if the insects themselves are not visible. A large number of adult insects leave soil or wood and discard their wings in a "reproductive swarm." If you see the swarm or discarded wings near your house, there is probably a large colony in the area. Also look for earthen tubes running from the ground to your

FIGURE 7–3
Differences of Winged Adult Pests

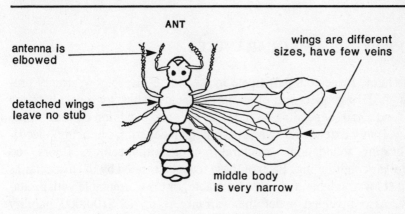

ANT

antenna is elbowed

wings are different sizes, have few veins

detached wings leave no stub

middle body is very narrow

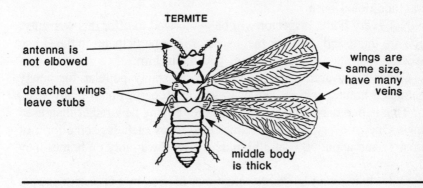

TERMITE

antenna is not elbowed

detached wings leave stubs

wings are same size, have many veins

middle body is thick

woodwork. Termites must have warm, humid conditions. They cannot survive in dry air, so to travel from soil over concrete areas, they build tubes.

Search for infestations in areas that favor termites. Pay close attention where there are cracks in concrete foundations, where the ground is moist and warm, and where wood is close to the earth. A common area for infestation is in basements, where dampness and poor ventilation are combined. Also check wherever wood is in contact with the ground or close to it—in your basement and under porches or steps.

If you discover signs of infestation, you should have a professional inspection at once—even if your real estate broker will require another one later. The longer you wait, the more extensive the damage, and the higher the cost of repair.

WARRANTIES AND GUARANTEES

Some home inspectors participate in the Home Inspector Warranty program. ASHI members will often make this available, for a cost between $250 and $350, depending on the size, age, and condition of your home. The warranty extends for two years and includes roof, plumbing, electrical, heating, foundations, structural framing, walls, ceilings, floors, and central air conditioning. Each of these features is rated by the inspector as being (1) warrantable, (2) not warrantable, or (3) warrantable with limitations. Also included under the warranty is up to $100,000 liability insurance. The warranty can be transferred to a new owner, or extended for an additional term.

Not every home inspector will be authorized to offer this warranty. If you are interested in it, ask the inspector if he participates in the Home Inspector Warranty program before you retain him.

General warranties are becoming increasingly popular for newly constructed homes, but are harder to get on properties built many years ago. This is one reason many buyers prefer buying new rather than used homes. One of every five new homes sold today includes some form of warranty, and about 90% of all builders offer a warranty on homes they sell.

Older home warranties are sometimes offered by real estate agents. They will usually cover plumbing, electrical, heating and cooling systems, as well as certain built-in appliances. But few include coverage for roofs, foundations, or construction. Warranties on older homes are offered by nationwide real estate firms, including Century 21 and Electronic Realty Associates (ERA), and by some insurance companies working through real estate brokers. Costs range from $270 to $400, and deductibles range from $50 to $100.

A warranty is advisable if your home is more than 10 years old, or if you undertake a major remodeling job in preparation for the sale. Most types of warranty are transferrable to the new owner, and being able to offer one is a strong selling point. The Home Owners Warranty (HOW) program, primarily designed for new home warranties, also offers a five-year warranty on remodeled homes. This warranty is provided through remodeling contractors.

Paying for a form of warranty is one way to eliminate or reduce the risk of potential liability if a buyer discovers defects after the sale. Some problems, though, cannot be insured or guaranteed, because the damage is too extensive. In that case, problems can be fixed only by spending money to repair them.

The relative value of different improvements you might undertake in preparation for a sale is discussed in the following chapter.

CHAPTER 8

IMPROVEMENTS THAT ADD VALUE

Many homeowners want to upgrade their homes once they begin thinking as sellers. There are times when improvements are advisable or even necessary; there are other times when an improvement can be an expensive mistake.

For purposes of this and the next chapter, a distinction is made between improvements and fixing-up expenses. An improvement is an expansion of a home's square footage, interior construction, appliances, or any other *permanent* change. Examples include additional rooms or floors, outbuildings, inside renovations, or conversion of a room or area from one use to another.

Fixing-up expenses fall into the maintenance category. These are usually recurring rather than permanent. Examples include painting, installing new carpets and drapes, and grounds maintenance. Fixing-up expenses are often cosmetic, improving the appearance of a home rather than adding to living space, quality, or comfort.

If you are planning to stay in your house for many years, you will view improvements to your house as a way to upgrade your lifestyle and comfort. But as a seller, you are more likely to consider spending the same money purely for investment value. There is quite a difference in these viewpoints. For example, the Anderson family had no intention of moving. But they wanted a family room and a renovated kitchen. By refinancing, they were able to afford the construction costs. They were not concerned with how the property's market value would be affected. They weren't planning to sell, and the reason for spending the money was strictly personal.

The Wellington family across the street made similar changes to their home. But their reason was different. They planned to move within a year, and hoped that investing money in upgrading the property would add to its market value and appeal.

REASONS FOR IMPROVING YOUR HOME

There are five main reasons to spend money to improve your home:

1. *To increase living space or comfort, when you are not planning to sell.* In this case, market value is not an issue. The decision is purely a personal one.

2. *To upgrade your property so that it is comparable to the average home in the area.* This might be necessary if your home is the same general size with a similar number of rooms as others, but is older, poorly maintained, or has other flaws. An improvement in this instance is probably not going to yield a profit, but the money spent on improvements will probably be recaptured, at least in part, when a sale does occur. For example, most three-bedroom homes in a town have two baths; a seller has a home with only one. Putting in a second bath removes a major flaw from the property, and will probably yield a dollar for dollar increase in market value, for the amount spent.

3. *To make an otherwise unmarketable home ready for sale.* Certain conditions demand immediate attention, and repairs are necessary. For instance, a house's foundation was weak on one side, due to erosion. The entire structure sagged, and an expensive repair was mandated. Without making this repair, the house could not have been sold for a realistic market value, if at all.

4. *To conform to local ordinances required of home sellers, or to fix a problem that a buyer will require before making a serious offer.* Many towns, cities, and counties require specific changes in older homes before a sale can be completed legally. This might be limited to ample power in the fuse box, grounding of electrical wiring, or smoke alarms. Or it could be more extensive and expensive.

5. *To improve the market value of a home* above *the average neighborhood value.* This type of repair is the most speculative. You might be tempted to borrow money and make a number of improvements, just to increase market value and make your home the most desirable one available to buyers. But if you are planning to sell in the very near future, this type of improvement is the least likely to pay off.

THE IMPROVEMENT PITFALL

Certain improvements make sense. If your kitchen is run-down and out-of-style, putting money into modern appliances, a new floor, counters, and improved lighting will make a big difference. As a general rule, buyers are most concerned with the condition of the kitchen and bathroom, so these are the most popular rooms for improving when expecting to sell in the near future.

If you have only a single bathroom in your home, your real estate broker might suggest adding a second bath before putting your house on the market. This is the one improvement most likely to improve market value *above* the cost of the improvement itself.

Most types of upgrades, though, will not increase the market value of your home by as much as you spend on the improvement. A number of nationwide studies show that even five years after an improvement is made, you will recover only a portion of the money you spend.

The averages all depend on market conditions in your area, and on timing. If you make an improvement just before a substantial jump in average home prices, the value of the improvement will also grow at a higher-than-typical rate. When home values go up, so does the value of improving what you have today. If the market slows down, market value might remain about the same or drop temporarily. In this case, your improvement dollars will not grow at the rate you might expect in a better market.

The interest rate on mortgages, supply and demand, local economic factors, and population trends in your region all affect how good an investment your improvement will turn out to be. One thing to remember, however, when considering whether to upgrade your home: If your motive is strictly to make a profit, think carefully before you proceed. You might spend $20,000 in the belief that the improvement will add $30,000 to your home's market value. But you could discover that this is an expensive mistake.

Figure 8–1 shows, on average, how various types of improvements add to market value after five years. Keep in mind that the values are averages only, and will vary by area.

The most profitable improvement is adding a second bathroom. This is likely to increase your home's market value by 130 percent—more than the cost of the improvement. Most of the other popular improvements will add only a fraction of the amount you spend.

EXAMPLE:

You believe that adding another bedroom will increase market value. You spend $22,000 (the lowest price in the average range). Five years later,

FIGURE 8–1

the future value of improvements			
IMPROVEMENT	RANGE OF COST	VALUE IN FIVE YEARS	PERCENT RETURNED
second bathroom	$ 5,000–11,000	$ 6,500–14,300	130%
renovated kitchen	$ 7,000–24,000	$ 5,600–19,200	80%
replacement windows	$ 5,900– 7,000	$ 2,500– 3,000	43%
replacement doors	$ 3,700– 4,800	$ 2,200– 2,900	60%
new bedroom	$22,000–34,000	$13,200–20,400	60%
new fireplace	$ 2,500– 3,500	$ 3,100– 4,400	126%
landscaping	$ 4,800–11,000	$ 2,500– 5,700	52%
new roof	$ 2,500– 4,000	$ 1,900– 3,000	75%
new deck	$ 2,700– 3,800	$ 2,200– 3,100	81%
solar greenhouse	$ 6,700– 14,000	$ 6,000–12,600	90%

your home is worth only $13,200 more. You have actually invested nearly $9,000 more than you will realize in added profits. This statistic is based on the premise that you will put your home on the market five years after completing the improvement. So if you put your home up for sale a few months after adding the room, you stand to earn back even less.

You must also be willing to recognize that you might have to spend money to upgrade your home, without regard to making a profit. Buyers might not consider your home a worthy purchase unless it has certain features—especially when all of the other homes for sale have those features.

EXAMPLE:

Joan Harrison converted her garage to a den several years ago. Her reason: The garage was never used to park the car, and she needed a den more than a garage. But now that the home is going on the market, the real estate broker points to the lack of a garage as a problem.

The den is an added feature that other homes do not offer. While that is a positive point, buyers will tend to react negatively. Whether they want space for storage, a workshop, or to park the car, they expect a garage or carport.

Joan solved the problem by building a carport. It required a building permit and payments to a contractor. But as far as the real estate broker was concerned, it removed the negative feature from the home as a marketable property. Now, buyers could appreciate the den as an added feature, not as one that took something away from the house.

IMPROVEMENTS AND MARKET VALUE

During the years you and your family have lived in your home, you might have made improvements for your own enjoyment. At the time, you did not think about moving or how those changes would affect market value. But now that you are thinking like a seller, what effect will those upgrades have on your home?

Here's a comparison of two homes in the same area. They were both bought in 1972 for approximately $30,000. Both homeowners made a $6,000 down payment, and signed a 30-year mortgage for the 80 percent balance. Both homes were sold in 1988.

The first home was not improved at all. It sold for $135,000, after closing costs and commissions:

Sale price	$135,000
Less: mortgage balance	– 19,000
Cash to seller	$116,000

The second home was upgraded. A second bathroom was added and the kitchen was remodeled in 1983. The owner financed the total cost of $19,000 with a second mortgage. The interest rate at the time was 15 percent payable over 15 years. The home sold for $148,000, after closing costs and commissions:

Sale price		$148,000
Less: mortgages		
First mortgage	–19,000	
Second mortgage	–17,000	
Total owed		– 36,000
Cash to seller		$112,000

Even though the second homeowner improved the property by $19,000, the net cash proceeds were almost the same. In addition, the improved property had a second mortgage, on which the owner had paid an additional $13,000—most of which was interest. It appears that the first homeowner ended up with a better deal. Net cash was greater on the unimproved property, while the other's out-of-pocket expense was greater.

Two considerations that modify this comparison are income taxes and personal attributes. The second homeowner's out-of-pocket expense is reduced by the amount of tax savings from deducting interest. The second mortgage expense is deductible, although it only reduces the difference by a few thousand dollars.

Of more immediate importance is the fact that the family enjoyed those improvements for several years. Was that enjoyment worth the expense? This question cannot be answered just by comparing the numbers.

As long as you own your home, any improvement you make should be made if you need it, or if you think your lifestyle will be more comfortable as a result. Looking ahead to sales profit is a mistake. No homeowner should be motivated by the potential for future profits.

Certainly, the value of real estate is widely acknowledged, and a personal residence will probably grow in value over many years. This is not in dispute. But because most improvements will be financed with a second mortgage on the home, you must not only evaluate the value of the improvement itself, you must also allow for the monthly expense of repaying that second mortgage. This adds to the cost of upgrading your home.

THE DANGER OF OVERIMPROVEMENT

If you are contemplating spending money to improve the home you plan to sell, be aware of average sale prices and types of homes in your area. A general rule to keep in mind:

The maximum market value of your home is limited to the range of sale prices for similar homes in the same area.

EXAMPLE:

You own a three-bedroom, two-bath, one-story home. During the past year, several other homes have been sold, with prices ranging between

$105,000 and $120,000. You estimate current market value at $115,000. You are thinking of adding a fourth bedroom, which will cost about $30,000. At first, the math looks good. If your estimate of value is accurate, your $115,000 home should increase to $145,000 by making this improvement.

There are two problems with this approach. First, the average new bedroom improvement will add only 60 percent of its cost to your home's value over five years. It will add much less if you plan to sell in the immediate future. Second, it's unlikely that you will be able to attract buyers willing to offer more than $120,000 for your home—even with the added bedroom. The combination of limited return on investment, plus the restriction of similar sales in the area, makes this idea a poor one.

Your thinking would be different if you did not plan to sell. For instance, you and your family do not plan to move, but you are expecting another child next year. Or you plan to open a home-based business, and will need that fourth bedroom for an office. In this case, your personal space requirements are priorities, and you are not concerned with investment value. You might view an improvement as a viable alternative to moving to a larger home.

Overimproving is an expensive idea—if you are doing it only because you expect to profit from them upon sale. If you change the characteristics of your home so that it does not conform to other homes in the area, you are not likely to profit. Typical modifications include an unusually large living room, addition of a second floor when other homes are single-level, or radical changes in architecture.

THE FINAL DECISION

Home improvements are popular. More than $50 billion is spent every year to upgrade homes in the United States. Upgrading often is less expensive and more desirable than moving.

This is true for homeowners, but not necessarily for sellers. One solution to this problem is to do your own improvement work, rather than hiring a contractor. According to *Practical Homeowner Magazine* (May/June 1985, p. 45), some repairs made by homeowners themselves will recoup more than 100 percent because their costs are much lower than a professional's cost. The survey reported:

Project	Do-it-yourself cost	Added value
Room addition	$12,640	101%
Bathroom renovation	1,540	172%
Attic conversion	3,950	138%

If you plan to do your own work, remember these points:

1. Most home improvements are more complex than you might think. Unless you are a skilled and experienced craftsman, you might regret starting on a major project, or even one you think is minor.

2. If you will need to finance your do-it-yourself project, you might find that lenders are reluctant to lend the money for it. Some will even refuse to take the risk.

3. The improvement will probably demand more of your time than you estimate. You must be willing to put in the hours, and your family will have to live with the inconvenience while work is progressing.

4. Consider the value of your time, versus the potential for the return on investment. You might do better spending the same time on minor fixing-up expenses in preparation for a sale.

The next chapter explores ideas for getting your home ready for the market. A few hundred dollars spent in simple repairs and maintenance could bring a fast sale at the price you want, and could prove more profitable than a major improvement.

CHAPTER 9

GETTING THE HOUSE READY

You can make a number of minor improvements to your property to increase its appeal and market value. Making these changes now could increase your home's immediate market value by as much as two dollars for every dollar spent.

As a seller, don't be surprised when your real estate broker comes up with a list of repairs you should make. For instance, you want your home to sell as quickly as possible, so you contact a broker. Upon viewing your home, the broker advises making a number of repairs as quickly as possible. By taking the necessary steps *before* calling a real estate broker, you control the budget and timing of repairs.

Another point in your favor when you take these steps in advance: You will make a better impression by preparing before the real estate broker's initial evaluation. There will be a higher initial estimate of market value, and greater enthusiasm from the broker for showing your property to buyers.

The real estate broker will look for flaws in your home that should be corrected before showing the house to prospective buyers. And on the basis of certain conclusions the broker draws from first viewing, an estimate will be made of the asked price. The higher the number of maintenance steps suggested by the broker, the lower that initial estimate.

Even though the broker's purpose is to get you the best possible price, the condition of your home will influence the estimate. If you begin this relationship with a poorly maintained home needing many small repairs, it will be more difficult to convince the broker later on that a higher asked price is in order.

No doubt, the broker will make suggestions beyond even the most thorough job you do. But by taking steps now, before you put your home on the market, you will save time later, and will also start your relationship with the broker on a more positive note.

CHECKLISTS OF ROOMS

Lists of ways to fix up your living room, kitchen, dining room, bathroom, bedrooms, and closets follows.

Living Room

1. Rearrange furniture to enhance the room's appearance.
2. Review color scheme of walls, drapery, carpets, and furniture. If the room is too dark, repaint the walls, add brighter wallpaper, replace dark paneling, or install lighter carpets and drapes.
3. Remove magazines, books, and other personal items from all surfaces.
4. Vacuum all floors and dust furniture.
5. Rearrange bookshelves and knickknacks to enhance the room's overall impression.

Kitchen

1. Rearrange pantry and cupboards to create a neat and orderly appearance.
2. Clean all appliances and sinks.
3. If appliances are not in proper working order, have them maintained.
4. Remove all garbage.
5. Check oven to ensure that all vents are clear of grease and odors. Clean or replace filters, ventilation, and exhaust fan.
6. Clean all counter surfaces.
7. Replace low-wattage light bulbs to make the room as bright as possible. For very dark kitchens, install track lighting.
8. Install new cabinets if old ones are worn.
9. Replace older cabinet handles.

Dining Room

1. Thoroughly clean dining room table. If needed, revarnish the surface.
2. Repair worn upholstery on chairs.
3. Clean glass on dining room hutch.

4. Wash and clean exhibited glassware and china.
5. Polish all silverware on display.

Bathrooms

1. Check tiles. Replace all that are loose or chipped.
2. Replace floors worn by water damage.
3. Caulk and grout tile joints.
4. Remove all grime, water stains, and mildew.
5. Thoroughly clean all surfaces.
6. Repair all leaky faucets and shower heads.
7. Clear counters.
8. Clean and rearrange medicine cabinet. Remove clutter.
9. Put out fresh towels, including a guest towel.
10. Check strength and condition of all towel racks. Tighten loose racks.
11. Install brass towel racks.
12. Replace worn shower or bath curtains.
13. Install bright light bulbs.
14. Check exhaust fan. Repair if in poor condition. Clean vent openings.

Bedrooms

1. Rearrange furniture to improve impression.
2. Make all beds.
3. Replace worn bed coverings.
4. Remove loose toys and clutter from children's rooms.
5. Open drapes to brighten rooms.
6. Clean nightstand and side table surfaces.
7. Remove personal items and clothing from all surfaces.

Closets

1. Install lights where needed.
2. Remove all storage and clutter.
3. Rearrange clothing to create an orderly and roomy impression.
4. Repaint inside surfaces if needed, to make closets as bright as possible.

5. For smaller closets, install shelving units to increase storage space.

Make a list of the necessary repairs for the rooms in your house, using a worksheet like the one shown in Figure 9–1. List the repair, supplies you will need, estimated cost of the repair, and a deadline. If you have a large number of repairs, the deadline is important. Organize your

FIGURE 9–1
Fixing-Up Checklist—Rooms

AREA	REPAIR	SUPPLIES	BUDGET	DEADLINE
living room				
kitchen				
dining room				
bathroom				
bedrooms				
closets				

schedule so that all repairs can be completed before you make your home available for showings to potential buyers.

CHECKLISTS FOR INSIDE THE HOUSE

Checklists for the garage, basement, and general living areas follow.

Garage

1. Remove all storage and clutter.
2. Clean floors, removing oil stains and dirt.
3. Sweep the entire area.
4. Store all tools and equipment.
5. Remove all spider webs, lint, and dirt.
6. Check washer and dryer, clean filters and call service company for required maintenance.
7. Clean appliance surfaces.
8. Remove all laundry.
9. Clear workshop area, putting away tools and rearranging for a neat appearance.
10. Check garage door for proper operation.

Basement

1. Repair sagging beams as needed.
2. Check for water damage, make needed repairs.
3. Investigate musty odors or smell of gas, make necessary repairs.
4. Rearrange storage areas.
5. Repair broken lights.
6. Inspect furnace, replace filters, and maintain as needed.

Living Areas

1. Repaint when wall and ceiling conditions are poor, or previous paint is faded or too dark. Paint in white, beige, or light pastels.
2. Brighten up dark rooms with tasteful wallpaper. Use brighter colors for accessories.
3. Repair loose or peeling wallpaper.
4. Replace shifted, loose, or deteriorated sheetrock or panels. Repair all cracks and holes.

5. Clean all walls and moldings.
6. Wash all windows and replace broken panes. Also replace all cut or rusted screens.
7. Check all windows for alignment and ease of operation. Repair so they work freely.
8. Check window moldings, and repair for water damage and age.
9. Check drapery, ensuring proper sash operation and replacing worn drapes.
10. Clean and wax exposed floors.
11. Replace creaking or loose floorboards.
12. Repair loose steps, check staircases for loose handrails, treads, or posts.
13. Clean carpets or replace old, worn carpets or rugs.
14. Check all doors. Oil to eliminate noises, tighten knobs and hinges, and replace worn door screens.
15. Replace all broken light bulbs, cracked lighting fixtures, or old switches and plates.
16. Clean all fixtures, switches, and plates.
17. Repair all inoperative electrical outlets and plugs.
18. Polish all brass surfaces.
19. Repair broken doorbell, and replace inoperative chimes.
20. Replace or repaint a worn front door to create a good first impression. Buy a new brass door knocker.
21. Check all locks, and repair or replace as needed. Install a deadbolt on the front door.
22. Check operation of smoke alarms. Replace batteries if out of order.
23. Put out fresh flowers.
24. Open windows before showing the home to air it out.
25. Eliminate all odors with air fresheners.
26. Open drapes while home is being shown to brighten rooms.
27. Remove unnecessary furniture from rooms to avoid a crowded appearance. Replace worn furnishings.
28. Remove pet bedding, food and water dishes, and litter boxes.

Attic

1. Check for leaks and repair as needed.
2. Reinforce or replace sagging beams.
3. Clear all ventilation openings.

4. Remove excess storage, reorganize for a neat and orderly appearance.

List the repairs needed for the inside areas of your home, using the worksheet shown in Figure 9–2. As you did with the rooms checklist, write down the supplies and estimated budget for each item, and set a deadline for yourself.

CHECKLISTS FOR OUTSIDE THE HOUSE

Checklists for the lawn, trees, plants, terraces, driveway and walkway, and exterior of the house follow.

FIGURE 9–2
Fixing-Up Checklist—Inside

AREA	REPAIR	SUPPLIES	BUDGET	DEADLINE
garage				
basement				
living areas				
attic				

Lawn

1. Mow the lawn, remove all weeds, and water regularly while your home is for sale.
2. If lawn is brown or thin, reseed or sod.
3. Cut back lawn from edge of foundation and house.
4. Cut back lawn from plants and trees.
5. Trim edges by fences, walls, walkways, sidewalk, driveway, and around plants, hedges, and trees.
6. Remove children's toys.
7. Put away all garden tools and hoses.
8. Repair loose or broken fences.
9. Repair cracked or loose retaining walls.
10. Clean up after pets.

Trees and Shrubs

1. Remove all dead limbs.
2. Remove and replace dead trees or shrubs.
3. Trim shrubs.
4. Remove overhanging or intruding limbs from walkways, gutters, and utility lines.
5. Rake leaves from lawn, driveway, and walkway.
6. Water regularly while showing your house.
7. Remove fallen fruit from the ground.
8. Cut limbs intruding from neighboring yards.

Plants

1. Weed and mulch flower and plant areas.
2. Remove dead plants.
3. Water all plants to improve appearance.
4. Spray for insect infestations.
5. Replace overgrown plants, trim for a better appearance.
6. Trim or remove all ivy and other growths from fences.
7. Remove plants too close to foundation, exterior walls, and vents.

Terraces and Decks

1. Remove debris from all surfaces.
2. Clear storage areas.

3. Restain, repaint, or seal all wooden deck areas.
4. Check railings, and secure loose ones.
5. Clear all spiderwebs and insect nests.
6. Wash entire area.
7. Resurface for stains or worn areas.
8. Repair all cracks.

Driveway and Walkways

1. Resurface stained and cracked areas.
2. Patch all holes.
3. Seal all asphalt.
4. Replace thin gravel areas.
5. Replace worn mailbox.

House Exterior

1. Repaint or reshingle if needed.
2. Check all shutters or awnings. Tighten if loose, or replace if worn.
3. Check gutters and downspouts for rust or leaking areas. Repair if loose or worn.
4. Clean gutters.
5. Check flashings around vents, stacks, chimney, and skylights. Repair as needed.
6. Check exterior lighting. Replace or repair if not working.
7. Nail down all loose shingles on house and roof.
8. Repair loose or chipped chimney mortar.
9. Paint all railings.
10. Repair cracks in foundation, walls, and steps.
11. Replace small, worn house numbers with new, larger ones.
12. Remove snow and ice from walkways and porches.

Prepare a worksheet like the one shown in Figure 9–3 for all outside fixing-up expenses. Set a budget and a deadline.

PROFESSIONAL HELP

The majority of repairs you should make are either cleaning or cosmetic changes, and can be done on your own. But you should never attempt to

FIGURE 9–3
Fixing-Up Checklist—Outside

AREA	REPAIR	SUPPLIES	BUDGET	DEADLINE
lawn				
trees and shrubs				
plants				
terraces and decks				
driveway and walkways				
house				

repair damages to your home's structure, to appliances, or to plumbing, electrical, and other systems with which you have no experience. Hire contractors and other professionals to take care of these problems. And for major improvements or correction of termite or dry rot problems, you will also need a professional—not only to correct known defects, but also to identify the problem itself.

A real estate broker will offer additional ideas for enhancing the appeal of your home, and for setting the right atmosphere. If you have pets, the broker will probably suggest removing them from the home while it is being shown. It may be preferable for you to be absent, too, so that prospective buyers will have the chance to speak freely with the broker while looking at your home.

Some brokers suggest cleaning a home with lemon-scented cleaners, putting on soft music to create a mood, or other ideas for influencing buyers. As long as these suggestions are not deceptive, take your broker's advice. Depend on the broker's knowledge and professional experience, and do whatever is needed to make your home as desirable as possible.

If you are present when your home is shown, don't apologize for any of its features. Don't try to negotiate with the buyer directly. And don't try to sell appliances or furniture. All of these matters should be handled by your broker directly.

In the next section, the methods of selling your home and working with a broker are described. You can do a lot to prepare your home for the buyer. After that, however, you must let the broker take over and work directly with the buyer.

SECTION 2

METHODS OF SELLING

CHAPTER 10

FINDING A BROKER

Over 2 million people in the United States hold real estate brokerage licenses. They represent sellers in approximately three out of every four home sales. The remaining 25 percent of homeowners sell on their own. According to a survey conducted in July 1985 by the National Association of REALTORS® (NAR), nearly half of the people who did not use a broker went that route because they did not want to pay a commission.

The commission paid to a broker can be money well spent if there is a high level of service and an acceptable sales price results. The same NAR survey asked sellers to rate the importance of four attributes. The percent that indicated "very important" in each of the areas was as follows:

Criteria	Percentage
Level of service	85%
Time to sell and final price	81
Reputation of the broker	78
Commission	30

So while the motive for not using a broker is often to save the commission, those who did use a broker rated other points as more important to them.

THE VALUE OF A BROKER

The broker acts as a buffer between seller and buyer. Negotiating when you are involved financially in the property places you at a disadvantage. Both sellers and buyers often are much more comfortable making offers and counteroffers through an uninvolved third party.

A second reason to use a professional broker is to achieve a sale within a reasonable amount of time. Most buyers go to the broker to find available homes, and having a listing with an active firm puts you in touch directly with the market.

Finally, real estate regulations are complex. The broker understands the law in your area, and will help you comply with all requirements of transferring title, disclosing the condition of the house, finding reputable termite and home inspectors, and filling out the massive volume of paperwork the sale involves.

A first-time seller will probably succeed without a broker. The NAR survey concluded that 72 percent were very satisfied selling their home without a broker's involvement. But 42 out of every 100 people surveyed also stated that next time, they would use a broker; one third were not sure; and only one out of four planned to again sell on their own. Although you can save money selling on your own, the amount saved is probably not worth the time and effort required.

When you, as seller, list your home with a broker, you create a legal relationship. In this contract, you are the principal and the broker is your agent. As your agent, the broker has a responsibility to make the best effort to sell your home for the price and other conditions you consider acceptable. That means showing prospective buyers the property and explaining the asked price and other terms.

THE EXCLUSIVE LISTING

The commission the broker charges is for finding a buyer, not for selling your home. This becomes an important distinction if you later decide not to sell. Most contracts between sellers and brokers specify that the broker's job is to find a ready, willing, and able buyer who agrees to your terms.

EXAMPLE:

You employ a broker and explain the price and other terms, and the broker shows the house to a number of buyers. One buyer agrees to all of the terms and makes an offer. But at that point, you change your mind and advise the broker that you do not want to sell. You will probably owe the broker a commission in this situation. The broker's duty under your contract was not to sell your home, but to find a buyer.

If this was taken to court, the verdict could go either way. It's impossible to predict how a case in any one state or county will be decided, based on the exact terms of the contract, your reasons for changing your mind, and other circumstances.

Under certain contracts, usually called "exclusive listings," you could also be liable for a commission to the broker if you sell on your own. The terms of such a contract usually specify that the broker is entitled to the stated commission if the home is sold—regardless of who sells it.

The exclusive listing runs for a number of months, which should always be spelled out in the contract. Upon expiration of that period, one of three events takes place:

1. Your property becomes an open listing.
2. Your property goes onto a Multiple Listing Service.
3. The broker's involvement terminates.

Some exclusive listings are entered jointly. In this case, two brokers each make their best effort to find a buyer and, regardless of who succeeds, they split the commission when the sale is completed.

If you are dissatisfied with a broker's effort, you can attempt to cancel the exclusive listing contract. You must be able to prove that the broker did not make a continuous effort to locate a buyer. If the broker has an acceptable offer at the time you want to cancel, or if the broker can prove an effort was made, you probably will not be able to avoid payment of a commission.

An exclusive listing is a good motivation for a broker to work hard to sell your home. Under this agreement, the commission is not split with anyone else, so the broker's potential for income is maximized. This is also an advantage to you, as the seller. The broker will probably make a sincere effort to sell your home as quickly as possible and for the best possible price.

If you happen to enter into an exclusive listing agreement with a broker who does not make an acceptable attempt to find a buyer, you have wasted time and might end up in a dispute about how much, if anything, is owed to the broker. When dealing with only one broker, you may be at a disadvantage if it turns out that the broker is not making an effort to find a buyer.

The exclusive listing is probably the smartest way to sell your home. You can avoid problems by taking these steps:

1. Shop around for a broker. Ask friends and professionals for referrals to successful salespeople.

2. Be sure you understand *all* of the terms of the exclusive listing before you sign.
3. Limit the term of the contract. Sign an exclusive listing for three to six months, but no longer than that. This is a reasonable period of time to find a qualified buyer in most markets.

OTHER LISTING ARRANGEMENTS

An open listing is a contract with several brokers at the same time. A commission will be paid to the broker who actually locates a buyer for you. You can cancel an open listing at any time, provided that no qualified buyers have been produced by any of the brokers involved. Under most open listing contracts, you also have the right to find your own buyer, and will not have to pay a commission.

In an open listing, you have several brokers looking for buyers, but you can also find a buyer yourself. These are advantages to you. However, the incentive for the broker is not as good as it is with an exclusive listing. With many people involved, a broker can make a best effort and still lose the commission to someone else. Many busy and successful brokers will not deal with sellers in open listing contracts, preferring exclusives.

The open listing contract should clearly state your liabilities. Make sure you understand the conditions under which you will or will not owe a commission. The contract should also spell out whether or not you will be liable for the broker's advertising and other expenses.

In most areas, a Multiple Listing Service (MLS) is available. Under this arrangement, your home can be shown by any MLS member broker. Homes might end up as MLS listings following a period of exclusive listing with one broker. Or, they might go onto MLS as soon as they are listed for sale, depending on the area and the going practice. Once on the MLS, a property listing is available to all brokers who subscribe to the service, and any number of potential buyers can be shown your home.

In cases where exclusive listings are not successful, a multiple listing does give you greater exposure. But it also makes your home very public. If you prefer a quieter way of selling, you're better off finding a broker with an excellent track record, and staying with an exclusive listing.

Before entering into any listing contract, you should thoroughly understand:

All conditions under which you will be liable for a commission.

The procedure and required notices for terminating the agreement.

The methods the broker promises to use to advertise your house.

Any broker's expenses you will have to pay, either upon completion of a sale or termination of the listing agreement.

The term of the contract, and your rights to cancel or renew.

Listing contracts should not be lengthy or complex. Read them all the way through before signing, but your final decision should not need an attorney's advice. Most problems with listing agreements have arisen because people did not take the time to read the agreement, and did not understand all of their responsibilities.

LOCATING THE RIGHT BROKER

Most sellers find a broker by asking friends, neighbors, or their banker for referrals. That's a good way to start. But you should interview at least three people before signing a listing agreement.

Avoid the hit-or-miss method. Don't try to find a broker by simply walking into an office and speaking with the first person you see. A successful broker is probably out in the field closing a deal, while the person sitting in the office is waiting for business. That's a sign of inexperience or a passive approach to the business. Of course, successful brokers must also spend some time in their office. But when you randomly select a broker to represent you, chances are you will get the least experienced, newest member of the firm.

Look for a broker who has been in the business at least three years, who has a professional license, and whose name comes to you from referrals. Speak with others who have recently sold their homes, your banker, and other knowledgeable people. Ask the brokers you interview what licenses they hold.

Also seek a broker who is willing to enter into an exclusive listing and who will limit the time of the agreement. Avoid agreements that will run longer than six months. Also avoid brokers who are newly licensed in your state, who want long-term exclusive listings, or who resist when you ask for references. A competent professional will promptly give you the names of other clients. A broker checklist is shown in Figure 10–1.

If you cannot find a broker from referrals in your area, or if you want to verify that a broker has a license and is in good standing, inquire with

FIGURE 10–1
Broker Checklist

QUALIFICATION	YES	NO
in business more than three years	✓	
holds professional licenses and designations	✓	
is referred to you by friends, your banker or other sellers	✓	
offers a limited-time exclusive listing agreement	✓	
has held a real estate license for a short time		✓
wants a long-term exclusive listing		✓
is not willing to provide references		✓

your state's real estate commissioner. This office is given various names in different states; the local office can be found in the phone book:

> *Real Estate Commission:* Alabama, Arkansas, Colorado, Connecticut, Delaware, District of Columbia, Georgia, Hawaii, Idaho, Indiana, Iowa, Kansas, Kentucky, Louisiana, Maryland, Mississippi, Missouri, Nebraska, New Hampshire, New Jersey, New Mexico, North Carolina, North Dakota, Oklahoma, Pennsylvania, South Carolina, Tennessee, Texas, Vermont, West Virginia
>
> *Administrator of Real Estate:* Nevada
>
> *Board of Realty Regulation:* Montana
>
> *Board of Registration on Real Estate:* Massachusetts
>
> *Department of Commerce and Economic Development:* Alaska
>
> *Department of Licensing and Regulations:* Michigan
>
> *Department of Real Estate:* Arizona, California
>
> *Director of Licensing:* Minnesota
>
> *Director of Real Estate:* Maine, Virginia, Wyoming
>
> *Division of Licensing:* New York

Division of Real Estate: Florida, Ohio
Real Estate Administration and Disciplinary Board: Illinois
Real Estate Board: South Dakota
Real Estate Bureau: Wisconsin
Real Estate Division: Oregon, Rhode Island, Utah, Washington

CHECKING REFERENCES

You should ask every broker you are considering for a list of their other customers. Of course, no one will give you names of dissatisfied customers. But by asking past customers the right questions, you can compare one broker to another.

When you speak with friends and other sellers, ask these questions to select the best broker to represent you:

1. How long did the house stay on the market?
2. How many people were shown the house before it sold?
3. Did the broker advertise in the local paper?
4. Were ads run continuously, or did you have to ask the broker to run subsequent ads?
5. What kind of listing agreement did you have, and how long did it last?
6. What was your original asked price, and the final sales price?
7. Were you satisfied with the final offer, or did you accept it because you needed to close the deal?
8. Did the broker help you through the entire closing, including instructions on completing forms and other requirements in escrow?
9. Did the broker call ahead for appointments, or show up with buyers unannounced?
10. Would you use the same broker again?

Remember that not all brokers are the same. Don't settle for working with someone who is new in the business, and who will become experienced at your expense. Knowledge counts, and the broker's professional abilities could make a difference of thousand of dollars in price.

A broker is a specialist at matching buyers and sellers, and the right broker will be able to demonstrate a successful track record. Any broker who also offers to counsel you on income taxes and finances should be able to prove they are qualified professionals in those fields. As you will see in the following chapter, you must be sure your brokerage relationship is defined and limited to the scope of services you need and expect.

BOX 10–1.
Professional Licenses

REALTOR®   This designation may be used only by qualified members of the National Association of REALTORS®, the largest association of real estate professionals in the United States. A REALTOR® has passed qualifying courses, subscribes to a strict code of ethics, and is involved in continuing education.

Realtor-Associate   A salesperson affiliated with a REALTOR®.

Counselor of Real Estate (CRE)   This designation is granted by the American Society of Real Estate Counselors, a division of the National Association of REALTORS®. The CRE subscribes to a code of ethics and standards, and specializes in consulting on real estate problems.

Realtist   A member of the National Association of Real Estate Brokers, who subscribes to a code of ethics and professional standards.

CHAPTER 11

SERVICES YOU SHOULD EXPECT

Real estate brokers, for the most part, do their jobs well. The National Association of REALTORS® reports that, based on their 1985 survey of home sellers, 69 percent of those responding would use the same agent to sell another home. While the record is admirable, you should understand what services to expect from a real estate broker, and what services the broker should not provide.

THE COMMISSION

The broker is paid for services by way of a commission. This fee is normally based on the selling price of your house, and the percentage should be explained in the listing contract.

The rate the broker charges is not set by law. When the broker quotes a commission, it's an offer. If you believe you should pay a lower commission, you can negotiate. The traditional 6 or 7 percent commission that many brokers charge is the standard fee, and most brokers will stand firm unless you can demonstrate that a lower rate should apply.

If you do plan to negotiate for a lower commission, be sure to do so before signing a listing agreement. Once you sign, you have agreed to all terms, including the broker's compensation.

There could be exceptions to this rule. Some brokers might offer to take a lower commission to prevent a deal from falling through. For example, an offer comes in below your asked price. The broker might agree to take a smaller commission to increase the amount you will receive if you accept the offer—a kind of compromise to help finalize the sale.

You should negotiate for a lower commission if the broker has a ready buyer at the time you enter your agreement. The broker will not need to advertise, nor to share the commission with another broker if your house is sold through a multiple or open listing.

If you offer to pay some or all of the advertising costs, the broker should accept a lower commission. The cost of advertising is normally factored into the full-service commission rate the broker charges. And if you are expected to pay for part of the costs that a broker would usually bear, you certainly deserve a reduced commission deal.

When you want to sell two or more properties at the same time, you might be able to negotiate an overall reduction in commission costs. For a single advertising effort, the broker stands to earn a double commission on a package deal.

If your house is very highly priced, a broker might also accept a lower rate. If the amount of money the broker will earn is substantial, a lower commission rate might be agreeable. For instance, 6 percent on a house selling for $100,000 is only $6,000. But if a house sells for $250,000, the same broker might agree to list it for a 4 percent commission. Upon sale, the broker will earn $10,000.

A higher-priced home will be more difficult to sell, however. Since there are fewer buyers who will qualify for an expensive home, the market is limited, and the broker will have to work harder to find a buyer. Your broker might refuse to lower the commission rate on a higher-priced home for these reasons.

Finally, if you price your home to sell quickly, the broker's job will be an easy one. Under these circumstances, a lower commission is in order (see Figure 11–1).

Rather than paying 6 percent, you can work with a discount broker

FIGURE 11–1
The Commission Rate

ask for a lower rate when:

➤ the broker has a ready buyer

➤ you will pay for advertising

➤ you are selling two or more properties

➤ the selling price is exceptionally high

➤ your home is priced to sell quickly

and reduce the commission cost to 2 or 3 percent. In this situation, you are responsible for advertising costs and will also be expected to see your own way through escrow (a full-service broker should help you complete escrow requirements). The broker in this case is compensated only for bringing the buyer to you. See Chapter 14 for more information about discount brokers.

THE BROKER'S JOB

Your listing contract will state that the broker will make a serious and ongoing effort to find a buyer for your home. The contract might describe this as "a continuous bona fide effort." This means that simply advertising your home or putting out a "For Sale" sign is not enough. The broker has a responsibility under an exclusive listing to speak with buyers and invite them to view your home, and also to go beyond merely showing the property. A sales effort should be expended. If the broker, in your opinion, does not make this effort, you may have a good reason to cancel your exclusive listing and locate someone who will try harder on your behalf. To cancel your exclusive agreement, you should check with your attorney first.

Your broker is also ethically bound to keep certain information confidential. If, for example, you list your home for $115,000 and tell the broker you would accept an offer as low as $105,000, it is improper for the broker to reveal this information to a prospective buyer.

As your agent, the broker's first loyalty should be to you. For example, a broker learns that the city plans to change the zoning of your land within three months, and that as a result, it will be worth much more than the price you are asking. An unethical broker might inform a buyer of this, resulting in a fast offer. The broker might even offer to buy the house directly, without telling you about the zoning change. The broker could make a fast profit from this. In both cases, the broker's actions are inappropriate.

An honest and reputable broker will also disclose to you all sources of income from the listing of your home. The broker should be working for you, not for you *and* the buyer. It's a conflict of interest if the broker is also receiving money from the buyer to locate a property (as a buyer's broker), to find financing, or for any other reason.

You should receive a copy of your signed listing agreement and all purchase offers and counteroffers submitted by buyers. In addition, the broker is required to deposit all funds received toward a sale in the proper escrow or trust account, including deposits made with offers, down payments, and payments toward closing expenses or inspection fees.

WHAT THE BROKER SHOULD NOT DO

A broker's job is to locate a buyer and help you through the paperwork required to satisfy requirements for a sale. But the broker should not serve as a tax or legal adviser. You should not expect advice from your broker about your legal rights or responsibilities in selling your home, the condition of title, or enforceability of a contract. For such matters, a qualified real estate attorney should be consulted.

The broker also is not an appraiser. A broker might have an appraiser's designation; but in the capacity as your selling agent, the broker should not set a price. This is especially the case when getting the listing depends on completion of the appraisal. A broker will certainly be willing to comment on the asked price, or even to suggest a price based on knowledge of other sales in the area. This is an advisory function only, and should be expected of the broker. The distinction is one of objectivity. The broker's opinion should be fair and unbiased, intended to serve you and your best interests.

The commission you pay to the broker can be shared only with an authorized person—another broker who deserves a portion of the total payment for bringing in a buyer. The broker should not make payments to anyone not authorized to receive money in helping make the sale.

The broker cannot enforce collection of the commission by placing a lien on your home. Liens can be placed only by contractors and other people who perform work for you with your property as security to ensure payment. The question of payment usually will not become an issue, however. In most areas, the broker is paid by the escrow agent from sale proceeds at the time of final settlement. Figure 11–2 summarizes the broker's responsibilities.

DANGER SIGNALS

While the majority of brokers have integrity in their dealings with sellers, there are always a few who do not serve the seller's best interests. Watch out for these danger signals:

FIGURE 11–2
The Broker's Job

RESPONSIBILITY	YES	NO
make a continuous bona fide effort	✓	
keep seller information confidential	✓	
remain loyal to the seller	✓	
disclose all sources of income	✓	
provide copies of all offers	✓	
give legal and tax advice		✓
appraise property to get the listing		✓
share commissions with unauthorized people		✓
place a lien to collect commission		✓

1. *The broker is in the habit of "letting you in on secrets."* For instance, the broker informs you that the buyer is anxious and can probably be talked into making a better offer. When a broker tries to convince you that you are being let in on information that's confidential, chances are the same tactic is being used on the buyer. The broker might be telling "secrets" on the other side. This sales trick is inappropriate for a professional broker.

2. *The broker argues with you about your price and other terms,* making it difficult or impossible to put your home on the market for buyers. If your price is unreasonably high, the broker should inform you of that fact. But the broker is still obligated to put your terms out on the market. Look for a broker who does not argue with you continuously.

3. *The broker tries to play the role of tax or legal adviser.* Be especially cautious when a broker represents knowledge in these areas.

It's a sign that the broker doesn't understand his or her primary responsibility—finding a buyer for your home.

4. *The broker does not advertise your home in the local papers*, or expects you to pay for ads while also expecting a full commission.

5. *The broker demands an unusually long exclusive listing (more than six months)*. Or, upon expiration of the exclusive period, the broker expects you to renew your exclusive listing even though no buyers were located.

6. *The buyers that do come through are clearly unqualified*. Either your home is too expensive, or they are only lookers and not serious buyers. A steady stream of people coming through is a sign that the broker is not screening carefully, or that every listing is shown to everyone, regardless of what they really need.

7. *You have an open listing, but the broker does not put up a "For Sale" sign or advertise the home*. The broker is trying to keep the listing as an exclusive, although others should be entitled to see it. When this happens, you're not getting the exposure an open listing should bring.

8. *The broker does not submit offers to you*. If the broker tells you, "You wouldn't want to even consider that offer, it was too low," insist on seeing it anyway. The broker's responsibility includes revealing all offers to you.

9. *The broker places a "Sold" sign on your house when there is no buyer*, or when an offer has come in but has not been accepted. This is a trick to prevent other buyers from making better offers (and keeping the whole commission), or keeping the listing as an exclusive when it should be open.

10. *The broker's exclusive listing runs out*. It reverts to open listing status, but your broker does not invite other brokers to view the house.

These 10 danger signs are shown in Figure 11–3.

A PERSONAL DECISION

The problems that some buyers have experienced in dealing with high-pressure brokers are the exception. The majority of brokers condemn shoddy sales practices and unethical behavior. You will most likely find a broker with whom you will be able to work with confidence and trust.

Be aware of signs of unethical behavior, and if your broker says or does something you are not sure about, discuss it. Keep the lines of communication open to avoid misunderstandings. If you want to question

FIGURE 11–3
10 Danger Signals

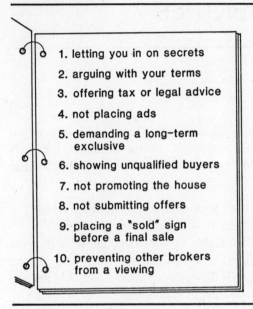

1. letting you in on secrets
2. arguing with your terms
3. offering tax or legal advice
4. not placing ads
5. demanding a long–term exclusive
6. showing unqualified buyers
7. not promoting the house
8. not submitting offers
9. placing a "sold" sign before a final sale
10. preventing other brokers from a viewing

a practice, speak with a representative at your local realty board or write to your state's real estate licensing and regulatory agency.

Even if your broker is completely honest and complies with the legal and ethical standards in your area, you might not be comfortable with the individual. When choosing a broker to sell your home, speak with two or three people who come highly recommended, then select the one who:

1. Is a qualified professional with a successful track record; and
2. Puts you at ease and answers your questions directly and honestly.

The selection of a broker is a personal decision. It should be based on ensuring that you receive the services a broker provides. In addition, you should be able to communicate well with a broker whom you trust completely.

CHAPTER 12

BROKER DUTIES AND LIABILITIES

Real estate brokerage is a complex business, and the people involved in it are bound by many laws and regulations. Being aware of the laws governing the practices of your real estate broker will help you as a seller in the following ways:

1. You will better understand your own responsibilities when you know the restrictions under which the broker operates.
2. You will know your own rights in your dealings with the real estate agent, and the limits of those rights.
3. Your awareness of potential danger areas in contracts and agency relationships will help you avoid problems.

The real estate broker must operate within the laws of real estate licensing, property, contracts, and agency.

REAL ESTATE LICENSING LAWS

The most immediate laws governing the practices of your real estate broker are your state's licensing laws. Each state has its own set of laws, and while overall principles are the same, the details differ from one jurisdiction to another, making it impossible to outline specifically how a broker operates in your area.

You might become familiar with the laws in one state and then move to another. Do not assume that regulations or practices are the same in both places.

All state licensing laws contain similarities. Every person acting as a broker must obtain a state license, and is required to meet certain qualifications. These are determined by administering an examination. Certain states require educational prerequisites as a condition of licensing. To keep a license in effect, brokers in most states must also engage in continuing education (by attending classes, seminars, or both).

States also require brokers to follow standards regarding ethics and the practice of brokerage. Licenses are granted for a limited period of time, and must be renewed periodically. This gives the state the opportunity to monitor broker practices and, if necessary, to not grant a renewal.

The state agency also has the power to regulate the industry. It investigates complaints by consumers or local real estate boards, and can fine or suspend a licensed individual, or revoke licenses in cases of extreme or repeated violations.

PROPERTY LAWS AND RIGHTS

A second area of law that restricts and controls your broker's practices is property law. Your broker could not possibly be fully versed in this complex legal arena. It is constantly changing as new cases go to the courts. But a professional broker does recognize situations where questions of law should be addressed and resolved.

This ability to recognize potential problems makes the difference between an experienced and an inexperienced broker. Smart brokers will insist on an attorney's involvement when they are not sure about the seller's legal rights, duties, and problems regarding the sale of property.

EXAMPLE:

There is an ongoing dispute with a neighbor about the property line. This dispute has been going on for many years, even before you bought your home. This question should be researched and resolved before you sell your home, and will require the participation of an attorney.

EXAMPLE:

There is an outstanding lien on your property that you dispute, or a lien is discovered that you did not know about. In either case, transfer of title becomes a difficult matter. In some cases, title cannot be conveyed until the problem is cleared up.

Questions of title, boundaries, and other property ownership issues should be handled by a qualified attorney. Real estate brokers should not attempt to advise you on these matters, but should be able to identify problems beyond the scope of their knowledge and responsibility.

Real estate laws are so complex that attorneys specialize not only in real estate, but in facets of real estate law. Be certain that if an attorney's help is required, you pick one who is experienced in the right area.

CONTRACT LAW

Your broker will be assisting you in selling your home, which means you will enter into at least two contracts: the listing agreement with the broker and the sale contract with the buyer. If the same broker also handles the purchase of another home, he or she will help with a new purchase contract and mortgage.

You could enter other contracts in preparation for the sale, or as part of it. These might involve contractors, professional home or termite inspectors, appraisers, and an escrow agent. You might decide to enter these contracts based on discussions with the broker. For instance, you choose one buyer over another when two or more bids are presented. The broker can comment on the pros and cons of each offer, and on the strengths of one buyer over another, but will not advise you on matters of contract law.

EXAMPLE:

Of three offers, you must decide which one to accept. Your first impulse is to take the highest offer, but the broker points out that it contains a contingency. The buyer is still trying to sell another house, and the offer depends on it being sold. There is a chance the deal will fall through if the contingency is not met. You might decide to take a lower offer that does not include a contingency.

This is the type of advice an experienced broker can and should offer to you. But it is not legal advice, it is only based on the broker's experience. Do not overlook the responsibility to which you are bound when you sign a contract.

A buyer makes an offer and includes an initial deposit with it. This is called a "deposit receipt" or "binder." It is a binding contract, signed by both seller and buyer at the time an offer is accepted. It's not as complete as the final sale contract, but does obligate you at the time you accept the offer.

If you have any questions about an agreement you are entering, you should consult a qualified real estate attorney before you sign it. During the selling process, you will be writing your name on many documents. Be sure you know exactly what your rights and obligations are before signing.

Be aware of the following points of contract law before putting your signature on any documents:

1. *All real estate contracts must be in writing.* While a verbal contract is usually binding in most situations, some forms of contract *must* always be in writing, without exceptions. Real estate contracts are one example. The statute of frauds in each state requires a written form in order for the contract to be binding.

2. *A contract may be express or implied.* An express contract spells out all terms and conditions, while an implied contract depends on the intentions and actions of those who enter into it. The contract with your broker expressly states the duties of the broker during the period it is in force. This is an express contract. But the broker hires an inspector who, as it turns out, does an incomplete job of inspecting your home. The buyer later files suit. In this case, it could be argued that the broker had an implied responsibility to ensure that a qualified and able inspector would be hired.

3. *To be enforceable, a contract must contain a number of elements.* First, it must have an offer and an acceptance, mutual consent that represents a meeting of the minds between the two people. If a court determines that there was no meeting of the minds, a contract does not exist. For example, a buyer asks you how much you want for your house, and you quote a price. But no contract is drawn up. Unless you and the buyer actually put the terms into a contractual form, no binding contract exists.

Second, there must be consideration. That means both sides receive something of value. In a real estate transaction, you convey title to your home in exchange for an agreed sum of money. So when a buyer offers money for a home, there is no contract until you agree to transfer title.

Third, both buyer and seller must be able to enter the contract. They must be old enough to legally be bound (in most states, you must be 18 years old). Both sides of the contract must also be legally competent to be able to understand the terms of the contract. A contract entered into by a minor is "voidable," meaning the minor has the option of cancelling its terms.

Fourth, the contract must be legal and enforceable. So if you attempt to sell a house that you do not own, a signed contract cannot be enforced.

Fifth, the contract is only binding if it is entered into willingly and in knowledge of the truth. If one side misrepresents facts, attempts to commit fraud, or deceives the other in any way, the contract is not binding.

Sixth, a real estate contract must meet certain requirements not included in other types of contract. It must be in writing, and it must include an accurate and complete description of the property. A street address may be sufficient, but most states also require a "legal description." This is a full listing of parcel number, length and angle of the boundary, and exact location (see Figure 12–1).

4. *A contract can be either unilateral or bilateral.* A unilateral contract is actually no more than an offer. It becomes a contract only if the other side accepts the terms. A buyer writes to you, for instance, offering terms for the purchase of your house. If you accept those terms, the unilateral contract becomes binding. But if you do nothing, then no contract exists. A bilateral contract is one agreed to by both sides at the time it is created.

5. *A contract in which all the terms have been satisfied by both sides is an executed contract.* If some provisions are yet to be completed, it is an executory contract. Both sides must complete the required performance of the contract. When you sell your home, you perform by conveying title and completing all agreed inspections and other terms; the buyer performs by paying or financing the agreed-upon sales price.

LAWS OF AGENCY

Real estate brokers operate under the laws of agency. There often is a lot of confusion about who is the "agent" in a relationship with a real estate broker, partly because of the titles that real estate salespeople hold.

FIGURE 12–1
Elements of the Contract

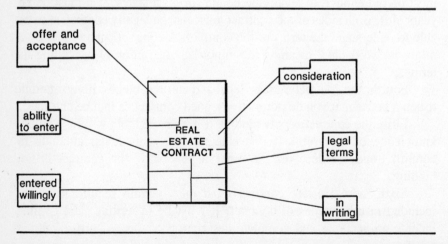

The term *real estate broker* describes the individual with whom you work in selling your house. In practice, that individual might be called a "salesperson," "agent," or "broker." If you retain a real estate *agent,* is that person your agent or the agent of the brokerage firm?

Agency relationships consist of a principal and an agent. The agent represents the principal for the transactions involved in an agreement. When a person owns a real estate business, that person is the broker of the firm. That broker might hire one or more salespeople and give them titles, such as "agent" or "salesperson."

The person working for the broker is an employee and, in one sense, is an agent of the broker. If that salesperson makes a mistake, the brokerage firm and its principal could be liable for damages. That same salesperson is also *your* agent, and you are the principal in the arrangement. This is the agency relationship that most concerns you as a seller. The legal and contractual rights you hold are dictated by the agency agreement you have with the brokerage firm. The firm is your agent, regardless of whether you work with the president or a newly hired salesperson.

You are the principal and the real estate broker is your agent, and you will be responsible for paying the commission resulting from a successful sale. But the agency relationship also extends to the buyer.

A real estate broker has an agency responsibility to disclose important and material facts to the buyer, to submit offers, and to show the buyer properties that suit the buyer's needs. These responsibilities are involved in the agency activities the broker undertakes, even though no written agency agreement is entered.

A person can perform as an agent is several ways. A *universal agent* represents the principal in all matters, including the right to commit the principal in a contract. A universal agency agreement is also known as power of attorney.

A *general agent* represents the principal only in a specified range of matters. Within that range, the agent can sign contracts for the principal and make legal commitments.

A *special agent* represents the principal only in one action or matter. This is the type of agency agreement you enter with a real estate broker. Under the terms of this agreement, the agent (broker) seeks a buyer for the property you sell, but cannot sign a contract for you or otherwise commit you to any agreement.

The agency relationship is created when you sign a listing agreement. If you sign an open listing, you are still the principal, but a number of real estate brokers act jointly as your agent. Any one of them may find a buyer and, by their separate agreement, the commission is split between the listing broker and the broker who actually brings in a buyer.

The combination of licensing, property, contract, and agency law defines specifically how a real estate broker can act in your behalf. These laws define your rights and responsibilities, and protect you from the dangers that could arise if someone acts outside of their scope of responsibilities.

CHAPTER 13

NEGOTIATING THE COMMISSION

Even with a legitimate reason and a strong argument for a reduced commission, you might encounter problems when you suggest a discounted rate to a real estate broker. There are several reasons for this:

1. Commission rates are standardized in most communities. Deviating from the acceptable 6 to 7 percent that most sellers pay is unusual.
2. Your arguments must be specific. You must convince the broker that the sales job will be easier, the property will sell quickly, or that the standard rate is too high in your case.
3. Brokers know that most home sales will yield the standard rate. They probably won't work as hard for reduced compensation.

SHOPPING FOR RATES

Most sellers never question the commission rate that real estate brokers charge. It's a widespread assumption that the quoted rate is never changed, and that it is set by law.

A national study released by the Federal Trade Commission in 1984 concluded that among sellers working with real estate brokers, 96.3 percent pay a commission calculated as a percentage of the sales price. And in nearly 9 out of every 10 cases, that rate was either 6 or 7 percent.

The actual rate in your area depends on the strength of the market, specifically on the number of properties brokers have for sale. So the demand on the broker's time and efforts has a lot to do with the prevailing rate. In addition, commission rates develop as a matter of practice over time. In one city, 6 percent might be the typical full rate, while 7 percent is typical elsewhere.

You will probably not have much luck shopping for a better rate. You will find that every legitimate brokerage firm expects the same commission percentage for listing your home. In fact, if a broker does offer to undercut the competition, you should probably wonder why. Since this is not common practice, an attractive rate could be a sign that the brokerage firm won't be willing or able to give you the level of service you expect.

One reason commissions are so standard is that most homes—90 percent—are sold through Multiple Listing Services (MLS). Therefore, many brokers have the opportunity to sell homes, regardless of the original listing broker. This tends to standardize rates. For example, the going rate in one city is 7 percent. Several homes go into the local MLS one month at the 7 percent rate. But one firm has a number of listings on which the rate is only 5 percent.

When a nonlisting broker brings in the buyer, the commission is split between the listing and the selling broker. So for brokers accustomed to splitting the higher, standard rate, the lower rate properties are less attractive. They will get only 2.5 percent, instead of the usual 3.5 percent. That's a reduction in their earnings of more than 28 percent.

Thus, other brokers will be unlikely to bring as many buyers to the property on which a lower rate is being paid. They can earn more money by showing homes on which the prevailing rate is in effect. This does not mean real estate brokers are unethical or dishonest, only that they are human. Whenever an individual is paid by way of commissions, they are attracted to the higher rates.

THE LOYALTY ISSUE

An unusual situation should bring about a lower commission. When you know there will be an immediate sale, when a buyer is already present, or when the house is truly priced as a bargain, you might be able to easily cut one or two percentage points from the local rate. But you should also be aware of how a reduced commission affects the broker's loyalty.

The broker works for the seller. However, brokers also have a duty to show the buyer all of the properties suitable for that buyer. Chances are, your real estate broker will spend more time with buyers than they spend with you. Loyalty is not exclusive.

A real estate broker does have to remain loyal both to seller and buyer. Since you pay the commission from proceeds at sale, the broker works for you. But because your sale price is probably set with that commission in mind, the buyer really pays the broker's fee, through a higher sale price.

When you argue for a lower commission, you may also reduce the time and effort a broker will spend showing your house to prospective buyers. A professional broker will still put forth his or her best efforts, but might work harder to convince buyers to consider other properties. As a result, you might *lose* time and money with a lower rate. Your house could take longer to sell, and you could end up reducing your price to attract a buyer—even to the extent that your net proceeds are less than they would have been if you paid the full rate.

The question of loyalty is made more complex by the fact that most buyers think the real estate broker is working for them. In the typical situation, the buyer approaches the broker and is shown a number of homes in a specified price range. So it's natural for the buyer to assume it's "their" broker.

Successful agents are able to maintain a balance between loyalties. They do their best for every buyer, and they also fairly represent the seller. In effect, they do work for both sides. But when the commission is reduced on one property, that delicate balance often is thrown off.

THE SPLIT OF COMMISSIONS

Before asking for a reduction in your rate, you should understand how commissions are actually paid out to brokers. It might seem that commissions are unreasonably high, and that the broker does very little work for what they earn.

For example, you sell your house for $90,000, and pay a 6 percent commission, or $5,400. The only time you see the broker is when buyers are shown the property, and when the closing paperwork is prepared. You think, "The broker only put in a few hours, and is earning more than $5,000. That's not fair."

The real estate broker probably brought through many people before a buyer actually made an offer you considered acceptable. You also have no way of knowing how much time the real estate broker spent with buyers in the office, representing you to the full extent of his or her ability.

If your home is one of the 90 percent of all homes sold through a Multiple Listing Service, and the selling broker was not the one with whom you listed, that $5,400 is split four ways. The salesperson who actually works with you usually shares all earnings with the broker. So the listing and the selling company are both entitled to a slice of the commission pie:

Selling broker	$1,350
Salesperson	1,350
Listing broker	1,350
Salesperson	1,350

If your broker works 10 hours to find a buyer, the commission represents $135 per hour. But that is not a realistic way to judge whether or not compensation is fair. Remember that the advantage of working with the broker is exposure. The broker is in touch with a lot of buyers and sellers, and matches them up as efficiently as possible. You could not contact the same market of buyers on your own, at least not as easily as when you work with a broker.

While your real estate broker might work only 10 hours to find the one buyer who makes an acceptable offer, there might be an additional 30 or 40 hours of screening and site inspections. The broker shows many homes and works with many buyers, only to have the sale go to a competitor. To be fair to the broker, the commission you pay is not just for finding that one buyer. It's really payment for the exposure and the efforts a broker makes on all homes for sale, and for matching up a number of possible buyers—even when that effort doesn't result in a sale.

The broker also has expenses to absorb, such as the gas and depreciation on an automobile, advertising paid to attract buyers to your house, office salaries and rent, and numerous other overhead expenses.

For the hours a broker commits in your behalf, the commission is reasonable. You are paying as much for exposure as you are for the actual sale. And the standardization of rates indicates that 6 to 7 percent is a fair market rate. If it was not, there certainly would be many firms offering lower rates for the same listings—enough to bring down all rates in your area.

Negotiate a lower commission if you have an unusually easy home to sell—because of an attractive asked price, the presence of a buyer, or in those rare cases when the broker offers to buy your home directly. But don't try to get a bargain just to save a few dollars. In the end, you might wait longer and lose more money than you save.

CHAPTER 14

DISCOUNT BROKERS AND FLAT-FEE AGENCIES

Most sellers enter a contract with a full-service broker and pay a 6 or 7 percent commission. A few prefer to work with a discount or flat-fee broker, under one of several arrangements:

1. A flat fee is paid just for finding a buyer. The seller is then responsible for negotiating the sale directly.
2. A reduced commission is paid, but the seller must pay advertising and other costs.
3. A flat fee is paid for help with paperwork but the seller contacts the buyer directly.

EVALUATING THE DISCOUNT APPROACH

No discounted arrangement comes free. If you expect to pay less than the full commission, you must either convince a full-service broker that circumstances make that a reasonable exception; or you must be prepared to do some of the work, or pay some of the bills yourself.

The most obvious reason to use a discount broker is for the lower commission. But if you consider all of the work involved in locating buyers, negotiating, filling out paperwork, arranging financing, and closing the deal, you must ask yourself if the savings are worth that extra work and expense.

EXAMPLE:

One homeowner expected to receive about $90,000 for his home. At full-service rates, he would pay a 6 percent commission, or $5,400. With a discount brokerage firm, this commission would be cut in half, to $2,700.

The arrangement called for the seller to pay all advertising costs, and no help would be offered with paperwork or with buyer financing.

A large number of buyers cannot easily qualify for their own financing, and brokers become involved. In many circumstances, a sale succeeds because the full-service broker intervenes and ensures that the buyer qualifies for a loan on the house.

Although the broker is employed by the seller, it is in everyone's best interests when the broker helps arrange financing. That could be the only way to earn a commission if the deal cannot be completed otherwise.

EXAMPLE:

A buyer made an offer on a house, and had the money available to make a 10 percent down payment. But the savings and loan association agreed to carry only 80 percent. The broker found someone willing to carry a second mortgage.

In some areas, a first mortgage lender will require a cash down payment for the balance of the purchase price. If the buyer has a sum of money invested and at risk, they're more likely to honor the mortgage. But in many areas, a buyer can borrow the extra money privately, and can even buy property with no down payment whatsoever.

Brokers often help buyers with financing, as that can make or break a sale. But a discount broker will not provide this kind of service. Service will be limited. For the lower commission, you will be expected to pay for advertising costs. You might put a daily ad in two or more papers. If your house is on the market for several months, advertising costs will add up. And there's no guarantee that the ads will attract buyers.

A second advantage often quoted is that, by paying a lower fee, you can reduce the selling price of your home. For example, you expect to receive $90,000. But if you pay a $2,700 rather than a $5,400 commission, you can reduce the price to $87,300, and still net the same amount. This should attract more buyers as the price is lower than comparable homes in your area.

There are two problems with the reduced price. First, you end up with the same amount of net proceeds as you would have received working with a full-service real estate broker—but you do more of the work or pay extra expenses while the house is for sale. Second, buyers are just as likely to offer a lower price for your home. You might end up with much less than you expected by using a discount or flat-fee agency.

A third advantage of the discount alternative is that you will reduce your contact with salespeople. In many discount or flat-fee agreements, you are actually selling your home on your own, using the services of the broker just to make contact or complete paperwork. The commission you pay is either a finder's fee or an administrative payment. For the advantage of limiting your contacts with salespeople, you also have the disadvantage of much less exposure to buyers. The pros and cons of using a discount broker are summarized in Figure 14–1.

Keep in mind that the greatest advantages of working with a full-service broker are:

1. Exposure to the entire range of interested buyers.
2. Advice from an experienced and knowledgeable professional.
3. Payment of advertising expenses.
4. Help with paperwork during escrow, and with locating financing for buyers.

If you want to save money on real estate commissions, you must be willing to go through the selling process without these benefits.

LIMITS ON SERVICE

Full-service brokers have an incentive to find buyers and get the best price possible. A flat-fee agency will receive a fee whether or not they find a buyer, so there is no pressing motive to locate a buyer and bring in the best offer.

FIGURE 14–1
Evaluating the Discount Arrangement

ADVANTAGES	DISADVANTAGES
lower commissions	higher advertising expenses
competitive price on your home	offers could be lower
reduced contact with salespeople	less exposure to buyers

With a flat-fee agency, the concept of "best efforts" doesn't always apply. The agency is not offering brokerage service, only a limited range of assistance in specific aspects of your sale. And a discount brokerage firm depends on volume. So they will not provide the same level of service as a full-service broker, nor will they spend the same amount of time working with you. It's simply not economical for a discounter to put in too many hours, since maximum income on each property is limited (see Figure 14–2).

A discount broker will not assist buyers in finding a willing lender, without charging an additional fee. If buyers are unable to arrange financing on their own, the offer could fall through. Most offers include the standard contingency that the buyer must qualify for financing. The offer will state that, if the buyer cannot find a lender, the deal is off. A full-service broker often intervenes to help the buyer find a suitable lender.

For many sellers and buyers, escrow paperwork is overwhelming (see Chapter 21). The experienced broker helps both sides comply with all requirements and meet deadlines during the escrow period. In most transactions, the broker is much more helpful and more directly involved than the escrow agent or attorney handling escrow matters.

FIGURE 14–2
Services Most Discounters Do Not Provide

√ helping the buyer
  locate financing

√ assisting with
  paperwork and escrow

√ advising you in
  preparing your home

√ contacting other
  brokers

√ referring out-of-state
  buyers

√ negotiating offers

When you contact a full-service broker, you expect advice on the preparation of your home for sale. Minor fixing-up expenses enhance the appearance and quality of the house, and the broker will offer ideas for attracting buyers. You cannot expect such extra help from a discount or flat-fee agency.

You have a considerable market advantage when your home is listed through a Multiple Listing Service. This broadens your contacts to every serious buyer in the area who is looking for homes in your price range. Some sellers find it distasteful to have many brokers showing their property, working with a multitude of prospective buyers. But this is really an advantage.

The large number of contacts obtained through a brokerage agreement is, perhaps, the greatest benefit of working with a full-service firm. You will not have this advantage working with a discounter. Discount brokers are not part of the MLS system, and a full-service professional will not be interested in showing your home to buyers for a reduced commission.

Some full-service firms are in constant touch with branch offices across the country. When a person wants to relocate to your area, your home is listed and available for review. Many buyers relocate from other areas, so your contacts can be national rather than local. With a discount or flat-fee agreement, you are unlikely to have the same advantageous exposure.

Full-service brokers act as a buffer between the seller and the buyer, conveying offers and responses until an acceptable price and other terms are agreed to by both parties. Discounters probably will not be willing to spend time trying to close the deal, and might require that you negotiate directly. A flat-fee agency rarely becomes involved in negotiations.

As a seller, you are at a serious disadvantage when you are required to negotiate directly with a buyer. You cannot be as objective as a broker, and, the final price will usually be lower because you are too closely involved with your own home.

MAKING THE DECISION

Look beyond the obvious savings in commission when comparing full-service brokers to discount or flat-fee brokers. Remember that the combination of advice, service, and exposure is important to you as a seller, and the full-service broker is more likely to already be in touch with a wide range of buyers willing to make offers.

If you are anxious to sell your house quickly, you will do better working with a broker who can bring in the greatest number of buyers, as soon as possible. And while you could cut some of the commission cost from selling your home, you might also have to reduce the price. If the reduced price is greater than your savings on commission, you haven't gained anything. In fact, you've lost, because you were required to pay many of your own expenses with a discount or flat-fee agency.

Take a realistic look at your property. How is it priced in comparison to other similar homes? Will it sell quickly, at a price near your asked price? Will a salesperson's involvement help?

In some instances, you can benefit from using a discount or flat-fee agency if you already know how and when your house will sell, or if you are willing to do a lot of work yourself.

EXAMPLE:

A homeowner agreed to a sales price with a buyer, and no brokers were involved. The seller and the buyer were concerned with details of the transaction, and they considered each hiring their own attorney to negotiate the sale. But because they agreed on all terms and their only concern was complying with the paperwork and legal requirements, they finally decided to hire a flat-fee agency.

In this example, the seller and buyer hired an agency just to consult on the paperwork requirements. The issues of verifying title, legally transferring the property, and managing the financial end of the transaction, were all organized by the flat-fee agency.

EXAMPLE:

In another case, the homeowner was in no particular hurry to sell her home. She hired a discount agency, agreeing to pay for all advertisements. She was firm on the price and did not actually place any ads, depending instead on contacts the discount broker had now and would make in the future. After several would-be buyers made offers below her price, one came along and accepted the seller's terms. A deal was finalized.

In this instance, the seller got the price and other terms. There was no rush to sell, and she was confident that the price was fair. A buyer was eventually found, and the commission was half the amount she would have paid with a full-service broker.

The cases when you will benefit from using a discount or flat-fee agency are rare. In most instances, the cost of selling your home is already figured in the asked price you set, along with an extra amount for anticipated lower offers. You might not really save any money at all by trying to reduce the commission cost.

Another alternative is to act as your own salesperson, and take care of the entire transaction on your own. If you take this route, be prepared to research the paperwork and title requirements before you begin. The next chapter explains this process in detail.

CHAPTER 15

ON BEING A FISBO

Many homeowners decide to sell their homes without the help of a professional real estate broker. These private sellers are often referred to as "FISBOs" ("for sale by owner"). The most common reason for going this route is to save commission costs. According to the National Association of REALTORS® (NAR), 48 percent of private sellers stated this as their reason for not using a broker. Another one fourth of private sellers did not need a broker, as they sold their homes to friends, neighbors, or other family members.

Whatever the motive for selling without a broker's involvement, you will soon find you still need help from an array of professionals; and that for the savings in commissions, you will have to invest more time and money in placing your home on the market and completing a sale.

OUTSIDE PROFESSIONAL HELP

At almost every stage of the selling process, a professional outsider must become involved. Most expect to be paid a fee for providing their services. When you use a broker, many of these fees are paid through closing costs, but as a private seller, some of these services require paying extra money.

Determine Market Value

The first step in selling your home privately is to assess the market value. Most sellers working with a broker depend on the broker's opinion, or on a combination of that opinion and an independent appraisal. If no brokers are involved, you will probably need to pay for an appraisal on your own—either as a first step or later, when you become involved in helping the buyer locate financing.

Set the Asked Price

Once you know the approximate market value of your home (often based on a comparison method of studying the trend in recent sale prices of other homes), you must set your asked price. It might be above or below the estimated market value, and is determined by how anxious you are to sell; how recent prices have moved; and what kinds of offers you get from buyers.

Some FISBOs invite real estate brokers to view their homes and give their opinions as to what the asked price should be. If you tell a broker that you intend to sell your home without help, it's doubtful that any will be willing to provide this free service. Brokers do give opinions about market value, but almost always in the hope that they will win the listing. So inviting brokers might be a fast way to discover professional estimates of value. But it's also deceptive, and is unfair to the brokers who depend on commissions for their livelihood.

Other FISBOs get brokers' advice when they first consider working through the traditional method of selling. They later decide to sell on their own, but can then use the brokers' opinions to set their own price.

Prepare the House

You must be prepared to perform cosmetic repairs to get your house ready for a viewing. In some cases, the repairs go beyond the cosmetic, requiring minor or major renovation. Unless you are a skilled craftsperson, many of these repairs should be performed by a licensed contractor.

In addition, you will have to pay for a termite inspection. You can anticipate a buyer's questions by having a thorough, independent home inspection performed. Not only are you legally liable for disclosing flaws to the buyer; you must also expect buyers to be more cautious and to ask more questions when a broker is not involved in the transaction.

Show to Buyers

At this all-important phase, you do not need any outside professional help. Here, you are on your own. But to succeed as a FISBO, you must be able to strike a balance between knowledgeable homeowner and objective salesperson.

Showing your own property can be your greatest benefit as a FISBO, or your most significant disadvantage. You know the good points of your house, and can enthusiastically sell it. But buyers will become uncomfortable if you push too hard. No one likes to view a house while an anxious owner hangs on their heels. While you will not be using an outside professional at this stage, you certainly need sales skills to successfully show your own home.

Prepare a Contract

Buyers may also become nervous when a sales contract is drawn up by the seller. The contract should be reviewed or even drafted by your attorney. A smart buyer will also subject your contract to review by his or her own attorney.

In most states, these precautions are not taken when a broker is used. There is a general assumption that the contract presented by a broker is legal, binding, and fair to both sides—and that all necessary stipulations are included. It might be advisable to have your attorney review any contract before you sign, either as a seller or a buyer. But as a FISBO, you must plan for legal expenses as part of the selling process.

Help Find Financing

One of the most valuable services brokers provide is helping the buyer find a lender. This is an accepted part of the broker's job, and is a function that helps both buyer and seller. Without this assistance, the job usually falls on the seller. if you want to sell your home, be prepared to find a lender willing to carry a loan for your buyer.

It often happens that to complete a sale, the seller has to carry a second mortgage for the buyer. For example, you get an acceptable offer that includes a 20 percent down payment. The buyer cannot qualify for the 80 percent loan sought from a lender. The lender offers only 60 percent based on the buyer's annual income. So you, as seller, agree to carry a second mortgage equal to the remaining 20 percent of the selling price.

This arrangement means you'll receive less cash upon closing, and also you'll assume the risk of carrying debt that the buyer might not repay. If you are forced to foreclose on the loan, the selling process becomes even more complicated. When a broker is involved, this situation could probably have been avoided. You might still be asked to carry some financing; but if you do not want to, the broker will often be able to make other arrangements and transfer the risk to someone else.

Without a broker, you will personally have to visit with the loan officers of local savings and loan associations, compare terms on loans, and find one appropriate for the buyer.

Title Search

Before transferring title, you must be able to prove that you hold it free and clear. So a title search must be performed. In many states, title companies do the search; in others, a title attorney becomes involved.

The buyer will pay the premium for a title insurance policy; however, as a private seller, it is up to you or your escrow agent to contact the title company and order the search at the right moment.

Closing

You will be on your own during the closing process, although an escrow agent might be helpful in instructing you and the buyer in the many forms and documents that must be completed, deposits required, and deadlines to be met.

When real estate brokers are involved, both sides usually depend on the broker to lead them through the closing. You will have to find an escrow agent and research what needs to be done. Then you will have to ensure that both you and the buyer meet deadlines and comply with every requirement of the closing.

If you sell your home on your own, you must research the many requirements in your area, and become expert enough to handle all of the paperwork and legal transfer documents. You might save many thousands of dollars on commissions, but you might also conclude that it isn't worth the trouble. Figure 15–1 shows the steps involved in selling your own home.

WHAT FISBOS SAY

The NAR surveyed people who had sold their own homes and found that 72 percent were very satisfied with the process. Twenty-one percent were moderately satisfied, and only 7 percent were dissatisfied (see Figure

FIGURE 15–1
The Need for Outside Help

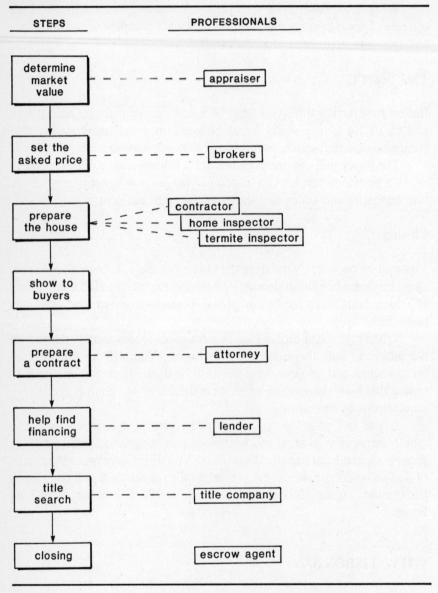

FIGURE 15–2
Private Seller Opinions

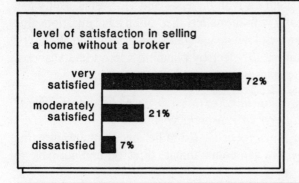

level of satisfaction in selling
a home without a broker

very
satisfied 72%

moderately
satisfied 21%

dissatisfied 7%

15–2). These results are encouraging for people who might consider working without an agent. But there's more to the NAR survey.

A large number of private sellers also stated that, next time around, they would work with an agent. This result (42 percent) probably reveals that the scope of paperwork, expense, and time involved in selling privately does not justify the savings in commissions. Only one fourth of the previous private sellers said they would go through another transaction the same way again, and one third were undecided (see Figure 15–3).

One of the intangible elements of selling on your own is dealing with

FIGURE 15–3
Private Seller Plans

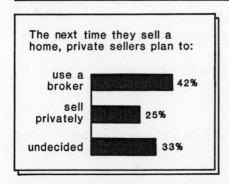

The next time they sell a
home, private sellers plan to:

use a
broker 42%

sell
privately 25%

undecided 33%

the buyer's perspective. When a real estate agent is involved, buyers understand the process. The broker is a go-between, a buffer who serves the sellers by matching them up with buyers—and vice versa. But when buyers have to deal directly with the seller, they often have questions that wouldn't come up otherwise. The buyers' fears are natural and should be anticipated. You can combat this fear by planning appropriate answers. Typical questions and responses are:

Why isn't this house being handled by a broker, like most others? Couldn't you find a broker to represent you?
I decided to not use a broker because I'd rather handle the transaction on my own. That way, we can communicate directly, and not have to pay a go-between.

Is there something wrong with the house?
The condition of the house is completely disclosed in this independent home inspection report.

Should I make an offer 6 percent lower than the asked price? That's what would be paid to a real estate broker.
The market value of the house is higher. I've already marked it down because no commission will have to be paid.

Are you so emotionally involved with the house that a too-low offer will create an unpleasant confrontation?
I consider this a business transaction. Any offer you make in good faith will be considered fairly. I've made the distinction between proud homeowner and seller.

Can you negotiate terms objectively or will the process be complicated?
I'll make every attempt to discuss your offer objectively. If you make an offer, we'll both be working toward the same goal.

You know more than I do about real estate transactions. How do I know I'm not being cheated?
This is the first time I've tried to sell a house without a broker. It's taken a lot of research, but I'll gladly share with you what I've found out.

These answers can be given even when the questions have not been asked directly. Assume that the buyer has reservations about working with you instead of a broker, and deal with those reservations in a straightforward manner.

SUCCESS AS A PRIVATE SELLER

The FISBO experience will be a difficult one if you do not prepare in advance. Remember that many of the services a broker usually provides are now up to you, such as:

Locating outside professionals at most stages of the sale.

Deciding how to price your home. If you set the price too high, it won't sell; if you set it too low, you will lose money.

Planning to show your home to buyers. A broker can coach you in some of the little details that make a big difference to buyers—such as getting rid of garbage, childrens' toys, and pet dishes, turning off the TV, and opening the drapes. When you sell on you own, you must plan these details for yourself. You must also decide how much or how little to say, what questions to ask, and how to communicate with the buyer.

Placing newspaper ads. How big an ad will you run? What will it say? How often will it run? In which papers? If your home takes many months to sell, the cost of advertising could be a major expense.

Setting your goal for the time it will take to sell, and for the minimum acceptable price.

Helping the buyer find a mortgage loan. This is an important service you will be expected to provide to the buyer in many cases, and the inexperienced homeowner needs to visit with many lenders and compare rates and terms before a serious buyer comes along.

Working with an attorney. You should ask for advice in drawing up a contract to transfer title, create a legal contract, and comply with all your state's provisions under contract and real estate law.

Figure 15–4 summarizes these points.

You might find the experience of selling your own home to be a completely satisfying one. But you must also be prepared to spend time and money to accomplish many of the services otherwise provided by a broker. A large percentage of past FISBOs would not sell privately again, even if they were satisfied with the outcome. Given the paperwork, financing, legal, and personal issues involved, many sellers would simply prefer to work with a real estate broker.

In the next chapter, methods of finding buyers are explained.

FIGURE 15–4
Self-Seller's Checklist

shop for professional help

price your home realistically

plan how to show your house

work out an advertising budget

set time and dollar goals

be ready to help arrange financing

use an attorney's help for the contract

Whether you sell on your own or through a real estate broker, you should be aware of the many ways that sellers advertise their homes. And you should know what a broker is expected to do to help expose your home to the market.

CHAPTER 16

FINDING A BUYER

Houses must be advertised in order to be sold. But some sellers resist the idea of placing a "For Sale" sign on their front lawn. The neighbors then will know you're planning to move, and other curious people might invade your privacy.

It is possible to sell without a sign. You can depend on a broker with good connections to arrange buyer appointments without a sign on your lawn. However, sales often result when buyers see a house for sale and then contact brokers.

The sign is also an important way for real estate brokers to locate buyers. They must constantly expand their contact with the market, and placing signs on properties brings customers. The sign on your lawn might sell someone else's house. And by the same argument, their sign might bring in the buyer who will end up making an offer to you.

If you decide to sell your home without a broker, the sign is even more important. Without the daily contacts with buyers or the advantages of a Multiple Listing Service, you will need that sign. Don't depend just on a newspaper ad to bring in a range of prospective buyers.

THE NEWSPAPER AD

If you are paying a full commission to a real estate broker, you have every right to expect that broker to place—and to pay for— newspaper ads. If you are asked to absorb any of this expense, you should also be given a reduced commission deal.

What agreement should you make with the broker? Be sure to include in the listing contract all of these points:

1. The frequency with which ads will be run.
2. The papers in which the ad for your home will be placed.
3. The size of the ad—number of words, size of type, and details to be included.

4. Whether your home will be included with other properties the broker has for sale, or listed on its own, or both.

Most sellers never discuss advertising with their broker. But if you want to attract the greatest number of buyers to view your home, you should ask your broker how this will be accomplished.

Ask your broker for the right to read ad copy before it is placed. A successful broker already knows which types of ads work best, but you should have the right to approve copy before it goes into the newspaper. With the large number of listings a busy broker handles, it's possible your broker will miss a feature of your home that is its best selling point. Every ad must have sales appeal, and should include (see Figure 16–1):

1. *A headline*. This should be designed to appeal to buyers in some way. Phrases like "priced for sale" or "clean" catch the eye. Depending on how your home is priced in comparison to other homes, the price itself might be the best headline of all.

2. *Number of rooms*. Every buyer has a specific number of rooms in mind, and looks through the paper for houses that meet these needs.

3. *Location*. Most buyers also know where they want to buy. If your ad leaves out this important information, many would-be buyers will not contact the broker. If the paper goes to readers in many communities, the city or town should be listed. In a local paper, the section of town should be included.

4. *Conveniences*. The ad should mention any special features that make your house attractive. Is it close to transportation, shopping, or schools?

5. *Features*. If your house has central heating and air conditioning,

FIGURE 16–1
The Newspaper Ad

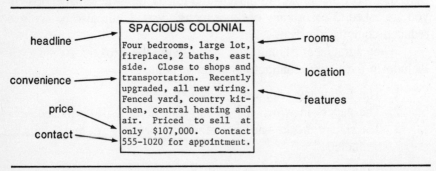

a fenced-in yard, a newly remodeled kitchen, or appliances, they should be mentioned.

6. *Price*. The price should be listed, especially if prices in your area vary widely. An ad that does not include the asked price is the least likely to get a response.

7. *Contact*. If you work through a broker, make sure the ad includes a phone number. And if you're selling on your own, include a notice in the ad, "by owner," and list your phone number and the best hours to call.

THE FACT SHEET

Brokers often prepare a property fact sheet, a summary of your home's features and the terms of sale (see Figure 16–2). This is useful as a giveaway during an open house, or for potential buyers.

A fact sheet can include extra features, such as the floor plan or a brief narrative section describing special attractions of the house. Fact sheets usually include the property's address, the broker's name and phone number, number of rooms, annual property taxes, asked price, and information about assumable loans. Also included is information about the style, construction, age, square footage of the lot and the inside of the house, room measurements, and which appliances are included with the house.

With a fact sheet, buyers who view many different houses have a good way to compare value for price and location. Without a fact sheet, buyers will not remember important details—and are less likely to make an offer.

THE OPEN HOUSE

The best way to show your house to buyers is through the open house. The broker usually asks residents to leave during the time buyers are invited in, and it's a good idea to take this advice. Buyers are less comfortable looking at houses when the owners are present. They want to feel free to criticize and discuss a home's merits openly. If the seller is in the room, they're not able to do this.

If your broker asks you to hold an open house, plan to be away. Also take these steps:

1. Thoroughly clean the house inside and out, so that people see it at its best.

FIGURE 16–2

---

fact sheet

address _____

city _____

broker _____ phone _____

total rooms _____ price $ _____
bedrooms _____ assumable loan:
bathrooms _____ balance $ _____
taxes $ _____ rate _____ %

style		room measurements	
construction		living room	x
age		kitchen	x
lot		dining room	x
size	x	family room	x
living space		bedroom 1	x
garage		bedroom 2	x
fireplace		bedroom 3	x
carpets		bedroom 4	x
drapes			x
deck			x
patio			x
heating			x
air cond.			x

appliances _____

_____

other features _____

_____

---

2. Open drapes to brighten every room as much as possible.
3. Make sure that childrens' toys, pet dishes and litterboxes, garbage, and other loose items are not in sight.
4. Remove items from overstuffed storage areas. Rearrange space to make it look efficient and uncluttered.

5. Rearrange furniture to accent a room's best features and give an open, spacious look to your home.
6. Remove all jewelry, cash, and other valuables from the premises. You cannot depend on a real estate broker to protect your belongings, especially if more than one buyer is on the site.

Sellers often resist the idea of an open house because they do not want strangers looking around. It's possible that burglars will case a house by attending an open house, and later steal your personal possessions. If you fear this might happen, you have the right to refuse an open house, insisting instead on showing the house by appointment only. This way, your broker can be more selective.

Another problem with the open house approach is that it is untargeted marketing. Anyone can attend, and a lot of people will come by who have no intention of buying. They may just want to see what houses offer in a given price range, or want to kill time, or satisfy their curiosity.

You can insist that your broker screen buyers before making appointments to show your house. If your broker shows to a large number of buyers over a period of weeks, but no offers come through, it means one of two things. First, your house is overpriced or has another problem that makes it difficult to market. Or second, if the price is fair and the house is in good condition, your broker is not screening well. Some brokers show every house they list to everyone, hoping for a match without doing any real screening. If you suspect this, speak to your broker. Demand that only serious potential buyers be brought to see your home.

Showing your home by appointment not only helps screen out the lookers; it also helps you and your broker schedule time. Most people who are willing to set a time in advance to see a home are serious about buying. They will make appointments to see properties in their price range, with the right number of rooms, and in the neighborhoods where they want to live.

JUDGING YOUR BROKER'S PERFORMANCE

The way brokers advertise your home tells you a lot about how well they perform their jobs. The best brokers match buyers and sellers well, and as a result, offers come quickly. Other brokers use the shotgun approach, exposing the entire buyer market to the entire seller's market.

If you prefer the more serious buyer and a limited number of walk-throughs, explain this to your broker. When selecting a broker, specify that you expect screening, so that your home is shown only to those buyers who will qualify for financing and who are seeking a home like yours. If you have made this clear, you can later correct a situation if the broker does not honor your request.

You have the right to refuse appointments. If your broker does not respect your wishes about the type of buyer, or if the volume is simply too great, take these steps:

1. Always talk to your broker first. Many problems of style and approach can be resolved if you keep the lines of communication open.
2. If your broker is not cooperating, speak to the owner of the brokerage firm. Ask for a new salesperson if it's the only way to solve the problem.
3. Refuse to admit anyone your broker brings to your home without first calling for an appointment.
4. Allow the broker to hold an open house if you're comfortable with that approach. But make sure that an experienced salesperson will be on site, and not the newest, least experienced one in the firm.
5. When your broker calls for an appointment, do some screening on your own. How much does the broker know about the people? Are they likely to qualify for financing? Are they looking for a home in your price range, in your area, and with the number of rooms in your house? If the broker has not first asked these questions of the buyer, refuse the appointment.

The difficult problem of selling in a buyer's market is explained in the following chapter. Special techniques will be needed to promote your house when there are more properties than buyers.

CHAPTER 17

SELLING IN A BUYER'S MARKET

When you begin preparing yourself to sell your home, you take many steps. The house itself must be put in order, repaired, priced, and a good real estate broker located. You have an idea of where you will move, and when you'd like to close the transaction. But what if you cannot attract a buyer?

The condition of the market today will determine not only the price of your home, but how quickly you will be able to sell it. This becomes a critical concern if you must complete the deal by a deadline. For instance, if you are being relocated by your employer, you will be most concerned with finding a buyer as soon as possible, putting the details of selling behind you, and settling into your new home.

CONDITIONS OF A BUYER'S MARKET

Before placing your home on the market, you should be aware of the current real estate situation. If there is a crowd of buyers waiting for homes to become vacant, you will certainly be able to command a higher price and find a buyer quickly. But if there are more properties than the demand, you face a very different situation.

An informed seller will know ahead of time how to price and market a home. Your real estate broker should be of tremendous help in appraising the current condition of the housing market in your area. However, you can find out a lot on your own, even before you retain a broker.

To determine supply and demand, sales trends, and conditions in the finance markets, you can ask for information from the following sources:

1. *Real estate brokers.* As part of your search for the right broker, ask for specific sales statistics. A broker who does not know this information is of little use, both in this initial phase and later, as your representative. You must wonder, if the real estate broker does not know the condition of the market, how can he or she serve you well?

2. *Local chambers of commerce, building exchanges, home builders' associations, and other trade groups.*

3. *Your banker.* Banks and savings and loan associations are in the mortgage business, and a loan officer will be most familiar with the condition in your town.

You may determine trends on a state or national basis, but these are of little value to you. Given the isolated segments of population and employment trends, supply and demand is a very local issue. Conditions in one area can be completely opposite those of communities less than 50 miles away.

EXAMPLE:

The counties surrounding a major city have very high levels of demand for housing, and prices have been climbing steadily for many years. But one county removed, property values are low, there is very little demand, and a low rate of turnover. Virtually no new construction is occurring, and houses take many months to sell.

The reasons? A major factor is location. People who work in the city want to live in surbuban settings, but still want a short commute. So being close to the city is desirable and drives up property values. Other economic and financial realities can further affect the market, but location is one important point that cannot be ignored.

Check statistics in your area. Become a knowledgeable seller before you think about setting an asked price for your home. Also consider how anxious you are to sell. It might be necessary to lower your price or to take other steps to encourage buyers and meet your deadline.

STATISTICS TO GATHER

Most of the information you need is available from a cooperative loan officer. This individual will know all about housing trends, market values, and the supply and demand factors that are important to you.

You must determine the kind of market in which you will be trying to sell your house. If there are 800 homes for sale, and only 300 buyers, you face difficulties. Buyers can pick and choose, looking for bargains and negotiating for exactly the type of home they want. If the numbers are reversed, however, your home will be very much in demand. Buyers will take what they can get, and will compete with one another by offering higher prices and other terms.

The first statistics to gather is the current supply and demand condition. There are two critical factors (see Figure 17–1):

1. *The number of homes for sale.* Construct a chart for the last 6 to 12 months, showing the actual number of homes that were on the market in your area. You can define "area" as your city, county, or neighborhood—depending on population, number of home sites, and volume of turnover in ownership. The larger your base, the more depend-

FIGURE 17–1
Supply and Demand Trends

number of homes for sale

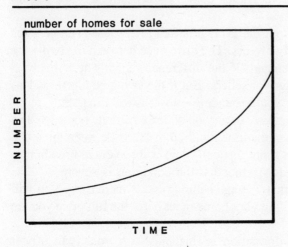

rate of new home construction

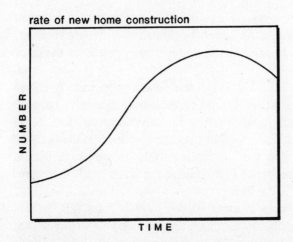

able the trend you develop. But the greater the area, the less accurately that trend will apply to your home and specific neighborhood.

If the number of homes is on the upswing, it could be a sign that there is excess supply. Of course, this statistic must be evaluated in light of other information you will gather (sales trends).

2. *The rate of new home construction.* If the volume of new home construction is on the rise, there has been buyer demand in the recent past. But if the trend swings up, and then begins to fall, it shows that developers can no longer profitably build more homes. Obviously, buyer demand is tapering off.

The second statistic to gather concerns sales trends (see Figure 17–2):

1. *The swing.* Find out the average asked prices and average sales prices for the last one or two years. The difference between the two—the swing—is the level of demand. If the difference remains at or below 5 percent, it is a positive sign for sellers. But if the swing begins to widen, and exceeds 10 percent, you're heading into a buyer's market.

2. *Months on the market.* In a good seller's market, homes sell in three months or less. When the time required to sell is between three and six months, the market is more difficult. And if the average time homes are on the market exceeds six months, the condition is severe.

If you spot a trend that average selling time is increasing, you will encounter difficulty in selling your home quickly for the full price you are asking.

The third type of information is financial. Ask your loan officer about (see Figure 17–3):

1. *Mortgage interest rates.* There is a direct relationship between interest rates and home prices. As buyers begin to demand more housing, interest rates go up. The demand for mortgage money increases the price of borrowing.

When interest rates fall, it's a sign that fewer people are trying to borrow money. This is a difficult trend to measure accurately, because many businesses and individuals borrow for other reasons than home mortgages. And economic factors other than the condition of the housing market will also affect the current interest rate. However, a drastic decline in the current rate shows that demand for loans (and, therefore, the demand for homes) is declining.

2. *New mortgage loans granted.* When interest rates fall, people who could not previously qualify for mortgages will be able to buy homes

FIGURE 17–2
Sales Trends

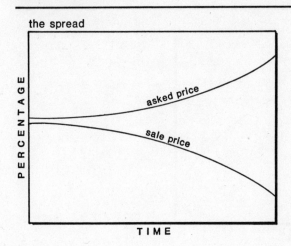

the spread

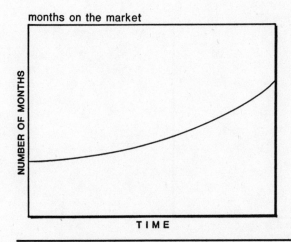

months on the market

as a result. With more attractive rates, home sales increase. So when the number of mortgage loans has increased over the past one or two years, there has been a high level of buying activity.

Once you see the direction of the trend, the favorable market might have passed. When buyers have made their moves, there are fewer new buyers looking for homes. This could be a signal that demand will soon slacken, if it hasn't already done so.

FIGURE 17–3
Financing Trends

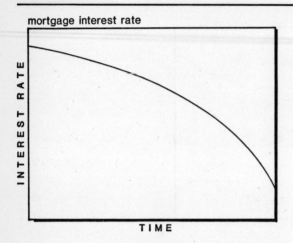

mortgage interest rate

INTEREST RATE

TIME

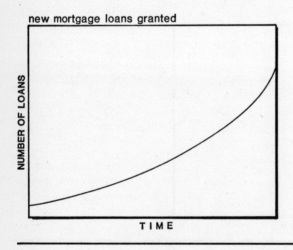

new mortgage loans granted

NUMBER OF LOANS

TIME

THE PROBLEM OF COMPETITION

When there are more homes than buyers, you have great competition. You have to compare the terms for your home with those offered by other sellers. You must also evaluate your broker's effectiveness and ability to attract the right buyer. If your real estate broker can show a buyer 5 to 10 homes in the right price range and location, your chances of an offer are reduced. So you must determine how to make your home the one a buyer will want.

The most desirable situation is to receive several offers at the same time. You can then compare the terms, and even eliminate offers that include contingencies. In a buyer's market, however, you will be fortunate to receive one serious offer. You might have to accept an offer that includes terms and contingencies you didn't expect.

ACTION STEPS

Be prepared to compromise in one or more ways when buyers have choices and you don't. You should take these steps in a buyer's market:

1. *Evaluate the asked price.* If your home is priced higher than comparable homes in the area, buyers will not make an offer. You might have to bring down the price so that it's in line with other properties.

2. *Carry part of the financing.* This is discussed in detail in Chapter 19. For now, be aware that you might have to offer to lend part of the money the buyer needs to afford your home.

3. *Offer to include extras.* Your house becomes a more attractive property if you throw in the appliances, fixtures, and even furniture for no extra charge. Small features like these are excellent selling points that a broker can use to interest a buyer.

4. *Pay the buyer's closing costs.* The buyer will be concerned with the cost of buying. If you offer to pay these costs, you will get a serious prospect. Again, this is a useful selling point for your broker.

5. *Upgrade the house.* Anticipate the features a buyer might see as negatives, and fix them now. If you can add a second bathroom, modernize the kitchen, or paint the exterior, you help make the house more attractive than competing homes.

6. *Evaluate the broker's performance.* Be sure your broker is working as hard as possible to bring buyers to you. If you believe the broker is not competing well in a buyer's market, discuss the problem. It might be necessary to release one broker and find another with a better range of contacts, or with a more effective selling technique. Be sure to consult with your attorney if you want to be released from a brokerage contract.

7. *Increase the broker's incentives.* You can inspire a broker to work harder if you offer a bonus or other incentive. You can agree to increase the commission by one to two percentage points if the sale is finalized by a specific date; or you can offer a cash bonus to the selling

FIGURE 17–4
Action Steps in a Buyer's Market

✓ evaluate the asked price

✓ carry part of the financing

✓ offer to include extras

✓ pay the buyer's closing costs

✓ upgrade the house

✓ evaluate the broker's performance

✓ increase the broker's incentives

✓ expand the open listing

✓ trade your house

---

agent in an open listing agreement. This will not always work, especially if your home is overpriced. Incentives also fail if the broker does not have the contacts or potential buyers for your property.

8. *Expand the open listing.* In a buyer's market, exposure is most important. Be sure your home is shown to the widest possible range of buyers. If necessary, offer an open listing to several competing brokers.

9. *Trade your house.* If you simply cannot get a fair price because there are too many properties on the market, trying to sell will result in a loss. You should consider working with a real estate broker who is in contact with a national network of offices. You might be able to find a buyer in a different state who wants to move to your area. A trade could work for you.

Figure 17–4 lists these action steps.

If your house is still not selling—regardless of whether you are in a buyer's or a seller's market—you must be prepared to take additional steps. This situation is covered in the next chapter.

CHAPTER 18

WHEN YOUR HOUSE ISN'T SELLING

You will experience difficulty selling your home when you're in a buyer's market. But other factors can make a specific property a "problem house" even when market conditions are ideal. If your location is poor due to noise, congestion, neighborhood problems, or other conditions outside of your control, the market value of your home is lower. It will also make it difficult to sell.

CHANGING YOUR PRICE

If you place your home on the market at one price and later reduce the price, you will appeal to a wider segment of the market. But reduced-price homes often are assumed to have problems, and selling them is still harder. Real estate brokers will be less willing to show prospective buyers your property if it's been reduced in price after being on the market for many months.

The longer your home is listed, the less enthusiasm you will get from brokers. Depending on commissions for a living, brokers will naturally want to spend their time showing homes that are priced to sell, with little or no problems in structure, design, or location.

If you believe your asked price is fair and your house does not sell within three months, identify the problem. Five possibilities must be evaluated (see Figure 18–1):

1. *Market conditions.* If your house is not selling due to competition, an oversupply of homes, or high finance rates, you will have to use techniques appropriate for a buyer's market.

2. *Problems with your house.* If the condition of your house is a problem, be prepared to invest money to correct the problems. This means less profit for you, but the alternative is to stay where you are and live with the fact that you cannot market your property at what you

FIGURE 18–1
Evaluation Checklist

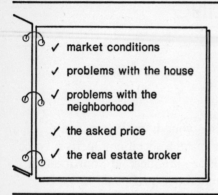

✓ market conditions

✓ problems with the house

✓ problems with the neighborhood

✓ the asked price

✓ the real estate broker

consider a fair price. For example, one homeowner could not attract a buyer because his home had only one bathroom. Virtually every other house in the area had two or more baths. People simply wouldn't consider the house seriously. The seller invested $12,000 to put in a second full bath, and sold within one month of completion.

3. *Problems with the neighborhood.* Your area might be undergoing a transition. Regardless of overall supply and demand, financing, and other cyclical conditions, no one wants to move to a neighborhood that's deteriorating. If crime is on the rise, especially violent crimes and property crimes, it is a very negative trend. If commercial outlets are infringing on residential neighborhoods, the area is considered undesirable. And if a large number of other homes are on the market because of these changing circumstances, you will have great difficulty finding a buyer.

4. *The asked price.* You might simply be asking too high a price for your home. If other properties are available for better prices, you cannot expect a buyer to make an offer at the price you're asking. The realities of fair market value might mean your home just isn't worth what you would like. The price should be reduced so that your home competes well with other homes for sale in your area.

5. *The real estate broker.* If you have eliminated all other factors, evaluate your broker's performance. Has the broker shown your home to a respectable number of prospective buyers, in your opinion? Is a reasonable sales effort being made? Is the broker running ads in the local paper?

If you determine the broker is not making every effort to find a buyer when there is an active market, meet with the broker and discuss the problem. If you are in an exclusive listing situation, you can ask to be released early, but you might have to suffer through until expiration of the contract. Ask for an open listing, consider looking for buyers on your own, or place your home on the local Multiple Listing Service.

SELLING ALTERNATIVES

Under the terms of most listing agreements, you have the right to sell your home on your own. If you do find a buyer, the real estate broker is not entitled to a commission.

If you have chosen to work with a broker, you will expect the broker to handle the selling of your house. If you have a problem with the broker's performance, you can certainly say that you intend to seek your own buyer. An exclusive listing is exclusive only to the extent that other brokers cannot compete for commissions. As the owner, you can compete with your own real estate broker. The chance that you might find a buyer could inspire a broker to work harder to sell your home.

If you get a release from your listing agreement, or if you decide to seek your own buyer, you increase the exposure to the market. As long as the other conditions (supply and demand, problems with the house, the neighborhood, or the asked price) are not factors, these actions could result in a sale.

Many sellers are under pressure to sell their homes as quickly as possible. Either they have made an offer on a new home, or have a deadline to move to another area. Trying to sell when you have already moved to a new area is a difficulty you want to avoid. And if you have made an offer on a new property, you face one of two problems:

1. The offer was made contingent upon the sale of your existing home. If you do not achieve a sale by the contingency deadline, the offer will fall through.
2. The offer was made without a contingency. You could end up owning two homes and being responsible for two mortgages.

You are at a disadvantage under such pressure, especially if buyers are aware of your problem. The buyers will offer lower prices, which could cost you thousands of dollars. Eventually, you will have to accept an offer, just to avoid losing your new house or ending up with the burden of owning two properties.

One solution is to handle the transactions separately. There could be a high demand for rental homes in your area, even when the market for home sales is slow. In that case, you can rent out your old house and probably cover your mortgage commitment. (See Chapters 20 and 28 for more discussion of this possibility). A summary of your alternatives is shown in Figure 18–2.

Becoming a landlord can also lead to other selling opportunities. Some buyers want rental properties, and will be attracted to homes already occupied by a tenant. Or, buyers who do not have enough cash for a down payment, or who cannot qualify for financing, often buy homes by leasing with an option to buy. In the typical arrangement, a monthly payment is made by the tenant, part of which is for rent and part for an eventual down payment. The agreement, which should always be in writing, should stipulate:

1. The exact amount of each month's payment that will be credited toward purchasing the house.
2. How that money will be used. It should be deposited in a separate account, in the eventuality that the tenant decides not to exercise the option to buy.
3. An agreement about return of the deposit. If the tenant decides

FIGURE 18–2
Selling Alternatives

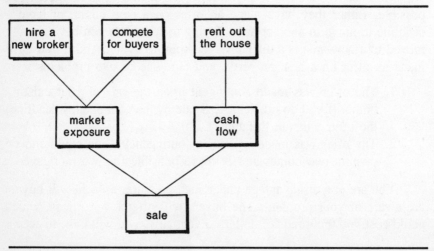

not to buy the house, the money saved toward a down payment should be returned immediately.

4. The specific price and other terms of the sale, if the tenant does exercise the option.

5. The date the option expires.

EXAMPLE:

You enter into an option to buy contract with a tenant. You agree that each month the tenant will pay you $1,200; $600 is for rent, $600 will be put aside toward a down payment. After 36 months, the tenant has an option to buy your house for $108,000. The accumulated deposit will be $21,600 at that time, 20 percent of the agreed-upon purchase price. The agreement states that the sale is contingent upon the buyer's being able to qualify for financing. You also promise to ensure that the house is in reasonably good order (contingent upon the reports of a termite inspector and a home inspector).

If the tenant does not buy your house, you agree to return the $21,600 immediately. And regardless of market value at the time, the option fixes the price of your home. If the market has changed drastically, and comparable homes are selling for $160,000, you are still committed to the terms of the option agreement.

This arrangement benefits both seller and buyer. You receive enough cash flow (from rent) to pay your existing mortgage, and also receive payments toward a down payment. The buyer is able to save to purchase your home for a price that is fixed at today's value, but has three years to decide whether or not to actually make a final purchase. Meanwhile, you will be able to move to your new home without the burden of two mortgages.

Lease option agreements should never be entered into without a written contract. Both you and the tenant should consult an attorney, and have the proposed terms of the agreement put in writing. In certain states, the lease option could pose some problems for you. If, under your state's laws, this arrangement is considered a partnership, you could be liable for *all* of your tenant's debts, which exposes you to unlimited liability. So it is important to check with a real estate attorney before entering a lease option contract.

A buyer—whether contacted through a straight sale, or as part of a lease option agreement—might make a perfectly acceptable offer, only to have it fall through because a lender rejects the application for a loan. In this case, you must decide whether to carry part of the loan yourself. The following chapter discusses this subject.

CHAPTER 19

SELLER FINANCING

A buyer who is having trouble qualifying for financing might expect you to help, by carrying part of the loan yourself. Seller financing—also called "taking back" a mortgage—can be problematic. If you need the money from the sale of one home to buy another, taking back a mortgage makes your own move more difficult. And there are risks. If the buyer is late making payments, that will in turn, put a strain on your new mortgage commitment. In the worst of all scenarios—the buyer defaults on your loan—you will have to undergo the process of foreclosing on the property.

THE FORECLOSURE PROCESS

In a foreclosure, you literally reclaim the house as security for the loan. A borrower is in default if payments are not made for a period of time. You have the right to take the house and sell it to get back the money you loaned. Other lenders have the same right, too, but only one loan has priority. Proceeds from the sale of the house will first be used to pay off the first mortgage. Then, if there is any money left over, the second mortgages and other liens will be satisfied.

EXAMPLE:

Someone buys your house for $100,000, making a 20 percent down payment. But because the buyer's income is too low, the lender, a savings and loan association (S & L), will not advance 80 percent and agrees only to lend $60,000. As the seller, you agree to take back the difference, a second mortgage for $20,000.

Three years later, the buyer is six months behind on payments, both to the first mortgage lender and to you. The S & L forecloses, reclaiming the house. Because the buyer did not maintain the property, the S & L has to spend $18,000 to bring the property up to marketable condition, and another $4,000 in legal and marketing costs. The house is finally sold for $95,000.

At the time, the lender's loan balance is $59,000 (loans reduce very slowly during the early years, and on a 30-year term, only a small amount will have been paid off). The proceeds will be divided as follows:

First mortgage	$59,000
Foreclosure costs	4,000
Fixing-up expenses	18,000
Total	$81,000
Remaining balance	$ 9,000

The most you can expect to receive of your $20,000 is $9,000—the balance is lost. The house itself was security for the loan you made, and it's unlikely that you will ever be able to recover the rest of your loan.

CALCULATING A LENDING PLAN

When mortgage money is tight and interest rates are high, you might have to carry part of the financing, just to sell your house. In the late 1970s and early 1980s, when rates were at or above 20 percent, it was very difficult to sell houses. People simply could not afford the monthly payments. In this situation, acceptable financing sold homes. The price was a secondary consideration. Anyone needing a house would pay the price if they could afford payments.

That all changed in the years that followed. As interest rates fell, appreciation of residential property also slowed down, and the market assumed more normal and orderly features. But even when the finance market is not as extreme as it was in 1980, you may be asked to take back part of a loan.

EXAMPLE:

One homeowner discovered that the request drastically changed her moving plans. Not only did the buyer make an offer $4,000 below the asked price; he also expected a seller takeback of a $20,000 loan. The asked price, $105,000, was to be used to pay off the existing mortgage, commissions and other closing costs, and pay for a down payment on a new home. The seller also expected to pay about $8,000 in moving costs. As originally calculated, after paying all expenses, the seller would have about $16,000 left over.

Under the revised plan, which included a $20,000 mortgage, the seller would have to come up with an additional $7,460 just to make the move (see Figure 19–1).

The seller in this case should not agree to carry a second mortgage above $12,000 to 13,000. And the full asked price should be expected whenever seller financing is involved.

It all comes down to a question of how desperately you want to move. If this seller has no choice, the offer of a lower sale price *and* a $20,000 second mortgage might have to be accepted. But if you think the price is fair, and are not willing to accept the risk of take back financing, the offer should be rejected.

If you are asked to grant a second mortgage to the seller, apply the same standards that any other lender will apply. A common mistake is to make the loan without checking into the buyer's credit history, income

FIGURE 19–1
Seller Financing Calculations

	ORIGINAL PLAN	REVISED PLAN
sale price	$105,000	$101,000
commission	−6,300	−6,060
closing costs	−300	−300
net sale price	$ 98,400	$ 94,640
mortgage balance	−48,100	−48,100
loan to buyer	0	−20,000
cash proceeds	$ 50,300	$ 26,540
to buy a new home:		
20% down payment	$ 23,000	$ 23,000
closing costs	3,000	3,000
moving expenses	8,000	8,000
total	$ 34,000	$ 34,000
balance available	$ 16,300	$ −7,460

level, and ability to make payments. You should ask yourself, if the first mortgage lender is not willing to risk the full loan, why should you?

Lenders will not lend money beyond the borrower's ability to pay. A popular calculation involves multiplying the monthly payment by four. If the buyer earns at least that amount per month, and is otherwise credit-worthy, the loan will probably be granted. But if the buyer earns less than the calculated minimum, the lender will reduce the maximum amount they will loan.

In this situation, a second mortgage places a greater burden on the buyer's financing. The first mortgage lender was not willing to risk the entire loan balance. Now, that risk is being shifted to you.

RULES FOR CARRYING A LOAN

Follow these guidelines if you decide to take back a loan in order to sell your house (see Figure 19–2):

1. *Evaluate the entire deal.* If a buyer makes an offer calling for both a reduced price and a partial loan, consider the total risk. You should be able to get full price, if you are helping out with financing. You should not compromise on both points.

2. *Check the buyer's credit.* Ask your banker for assistance in determining the buyer's credit history. Mnay sellers fail to get a credit report, which is not expensive or difficult to obtain.

3. *Set the right interest rate.* The maximum rate you are allowed to charge to a buyer is set by law. Find out what that rate is before you set

FIGURE 19–2
Seller Lending Rules

1. Evaluate the entire deal.
2. Check the buyer's credit.
3. Set the right interest rate.
4. See your attorney.
5. Include payment policies.
6. Set a short term.
7. Insist on a down payment.

the rate with the buyer. Don't make the mistake of charging too little. An extremely low-rate loan gives the buyer little incentive to pay off that loan before the due date.

4. *See your attorney.* Make sure you are in compliance with the law regarding rate and method of computing interest on your second mortgage. Your attorney should also draw up the actual note for the loan.

5. *Include payment policies.* Do not include prepayment penalties in your second mortgage, as lending institutions do. Give the buyer every incentive to pay off the loan as quickly as possible. And, if the laws in your state allow, include a provision for a late payment charge. If you do not have the right to assess this charge, the buyer has no incentive to make timely payments.

6. *Set a short term.* If you allow the buyer to repay your loan over many years—10 or more—your risk extends over too long a period. The shorter the term, the better. A buyer might simply be unable to afford accelerated payments on a three-year loan, so you might be forced to compromise on this point. But get the shortest practical term you can.

7. *Insist on a down payment.* The worst situation for taking back a loan is when little or no cash is put up by the buyer. For example, the first mortgage lender agrees to an 80 percent loan, and you are asked to take back the remaining 20 percent. In this case, the buyer will be putting up no money besides closing costs.

The more money the buyer invests, the greater the stake in keeping the property. And that means making all required loan payments. You should insist on a minimum of 20 percent down, just like a first mortgage lender. This also increases the possibility that, if the property is later foreclosed, there will be enough equity to repay your loan balance.

COMPUTING INTEREST ON THE LOAN

Figuring out the monthly payment on a loan you grant to a buyer depends on several points:

1. The method of computing interest (monthly, quarterly, semi-annually, or annually).
2. The interest rate.
3. The amount borrowed.
4. The number of years allowed for repayment (the term).

The monthly payment is calculated by referring to a book of amortization tables. These can be bought for about $5 in any bookstore.

The amortization table gives all the information you need to figure the monthly payment. Most interest rate books are divided into sections for the frequency of compounding, devoting one page for each rate of interest. An example of a table is shown if Figure 19–3.

Once you know the amount of each month's payment, you must figure a breakdown between principal and interest. This necessitates certain calculations, since interest will be higher in the earlier years, when the loan balance is greater. Interest is always computed as a percentage of the current outstanding loan balance. This procedure is shown in Figure 19–4.

These calculations are repeated each month, with subsequent interest payments becoming lower as the loan balance declines. For instance, during the first five months, a $35,000 loan would be amortized (paid off) in this way:

Month	Total payment	Interest	Principal	Balance
				$35,000.00
Jan	$424.65	$233.35	$191.30	34,808.70
Feb	424.65	232.06	192.59	34,616.11
Mar	424.65	230.77	193.88	34,422.23
Apr	424.65	229.48	195.17	34,227.06
May	424.65	228.18	196.47	34,030.59

FIGURE 19–3
Amortization Table

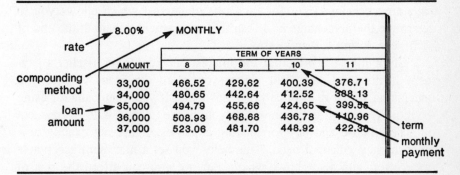

FIGURE 19–4
Dividing Monthly Payments

$35,000 loan, 8% interest,
10 years ($424.65 per month):

1. DETERMINE THE MONTHLY RATE

$$\frac{8\%}{12} = .006667 \text{ (per month)}$$

2. COMPUTE THIS MONTH'S INTEREST

$35,000 x .006667 = $233.35
(interest)

3. SUBTRACT INTEREST FROM TOTAL PAYMENT

$424.65 − $233.35 = $191.30
(principal)

4. SUBTRACT PRINCIPAL FROM OLD BALANCE

$35,000.00 − $191.30

= $34,808.70
(new balance)

The rate of amortization accelerates as the term progresses. In a 10-year loan, the balance is not reduced by 10 percent each year. Rather, it declines on a rate that increases toward the end of the term. This is illustrated in Figure 19–5. Most books of amortization tables also include remaining balance tables for each rate of interest which allows you to determine the percentage of a loan that will remain unpaid at the end of each year during a loan's term.

Computing the principal and interest breakdown on a seller's payment is the final step. But before you reach this step, be sure you understand all the risks of carrying financing. If your plan calls for using the money you will get from selling your house to make a down payment on a new house and pay for moving expenses, figure out exactly how much money you will need. This helps you set a minimum acceptable price offer, and also shows whether or not you can afford the risk of taking back a loan.

FIGURE 19–5
Remaining Balance

8% loan, 10 years

END OF YEAR	% OF TOTAL LOAN	
	UNPAID	PAID
1	93.2%	6.8%
2	85.8	14.2
3	77.8	22.2
4	69.2	30.8
5	59.8	40.2
6	49.7	50.3
7	38.7	61.3
8	26.8	73.2
9	14.0	86.0
10	0	100.0

If you need all of the money you expect from equity, do not accept an offer that includes a second mortgage. Wait for a better offer to come along, and leave the risk-taking to companies in the lending business. If you do decide to take back a loan, be sure you know the limits of what you can afford.

The upcoming chapter explains the timing of your sale if you are purchasing another house. Your plan for the use of money will certainly be affected by whether or not you have to take back a loan. Timing a sale with a purchase can also affect your ability to compete with other buyers for your new house.

CHAPTER 20

SELLING BEFORE BUYING

You will need housing for the rest of your life. So whenever you sell your present house, you must be prepared to move somewhere else. The timing of these events could create problems.

If you sell first and then look for another house, you will have to pay expensive hotel bills for yourself and your family. The time required to find a house, negotiate a deal, and close the sale could be two months or more—depending on the condition of the market.

Becoming a renter for the period of transition could prove to be a practical solution, especially if you will be relocating to another city or town. But that means moving everything twice, or putting your possessions in storage.

If you buy a new house before you sell your current one, you could end up with two properties. You will be responsible for payments on two mortgages, which many people simply cannot afford. You might also have difficulty qualifying for a new loan as long as you still have an outstanding mortgage on your present house. In this case, you have little choice but to sell your house first, and then look for another.

THE TWO-HOUSE PROBLEM

To avoid paying two mortgages, consider renting out your present home on a month-to-month basis. You might even decide to hold on to your house and convert it to a rental property (see Chapter 29). This benefits you in two ways. First, it eliminates the financial problem of paying on two mortgages. The rental income should be enough to pay your existing mortgage. Second, it removes the pressure you will be under as a seller. Having to sell quickly is a severe disadvantage for you. When you are in no hurry to sell, you have the luxury of considering many offers—not just the first one that comes along.

There are risks, of course. If you have a tenant who does not pay rent on time, you might be late with your own mortgage payment. And if the tenant falls several months behind, you might have to evict. In some communities, eviction is a time-consuming and expensive procedure. It is also difficult to manage your own property from a distance. If you are moving far away, you must figure out how to ensure that the tenant is caring for your house.

THE CONTINGENCY PROBLEM

If you must time the sale of your present house with the purchase of another, you can consider making a contingency offer. Under this arrangement, you make an offer to purchase a new home, but it's valid only if you complete a sale on your present home by a specified deadline. Contingencies might work in a buyer's market. But if you there is any competition at all, a contingency is not the best alternative.

Look at the problem from a seller's point of view. For example, you are asking $95,000 for your house, and you receive two offers. One is for the full price, but is contingent on the sale of a previous home within 30 days. The other offer is for $91,000, but includes no contingencies. Which one are you most likely to accept? Remembering that you must move elsewhere, you might be willing to give up $4,000 to close a deal right away, rather than risk having the other arrangement fall through because the buyer does not conclude a separate deal.

The decision about timing your move depends to a great extent on the condition of the market. If homes are selling fairly quickly, and yours is priced reasonably, you should not fear a long delay in finding a buyer. But if the market is slow, you might have to put your home up for sale, and then—once you have a buyer—find a new home for yourself as quickly as possible.

If you are moving to a new area, remember that the demand for housing changes by region. Homes might be selling very slowly in your area, but there could be a shortage where you're moving. You might have to stay in a hotel while you seek a new residence. But it would also be a mistake to buy first if you're not sure how long it will take to sell your present house. You could end up with a vacant home and two mortgages, putting a strain on your budget that you cannot afford.

When moving from one area to another because the job market is better elsewhere, chances are you will face this situation. There will probably be a greater demand for housing where you're going. So you will be competing with other people relocating and needing housing. In your present location, though, there might be a glut of available homes, and a relatively slow market.

SPEEDING UP YOUR SALE

When you want to sell your home quickly, you should be flexible on your asked price. Sellers who are willing to accept a few thousand dollars less than the asked price, close deals more quickly. You could start by establishing a lower asked price. But under many market conditions, would-be buyers automatically assume you'll accept less, and will not be willing to pay the full price.

Some people, in an attempt to sell their homes fast and still realize what they consider a decent profit, have unintentionally slowed down the selling process. For instance, you decide on an asked price of $109,000 with the following points in mind:

1. You will have to pay a 6 percent commission to a real estate broker.
2. You expect offers from $3,000 to $5,000 below your asked price.

You would like to get $100,000 for your house. But you set an asked price of $109,000 because if you receive an offer of $106,000, the commission will be $6,360. Setting your asked price with these considerations will allow you to get about what you expected.

The problem, though, is that by pricing your home much higher, you will decrease buyer interest. If potential buyers are looking for homes at or below $100,000, your property will be priced too high. You should be willing to accept a lower offer if you must sell quickly; but marking up the price can remove that advantage.

The solution is to set your asked price at a level in line with prices of similar homes and also know in advance how much you are willing to accept, as a minimum. For example, you would like to receive $100,000 after commissions, but you also know that the average sales price for similar homes has been between $98,000 and $107,000. By setting your price at $105,000, you will be within the range of recent sales prices. An offer of at least $102,000 would be acceptable, even though it is a few thousand dollars less than you'd like.

You must balance the desire for profit with a realistic appraisal of today's market. This means setting a price within the range of recent sales, and in some cases, being willing to accept less than you would like. The faster you must sell, the more you must be willing to give up in price.

SPEEDING UP YOUR PURCHASE

You have the best chance of finding another home with the right price and location when you can make a straight offer. A contingency offer puts you at a serious disadvantage.

EXAMPLE:

One homeowner relocated several hundred miles and made an offer on a new home. The asked price was $115,000, and he offered $112,000, with a contingency. The owner responded that with the contingency, the full price was firm.

There was a choice. Either offer the full price, or remove the contingency. If the seller of the new house was having trouble finding buyers, you might get away with a contingency and a reduced-price offer. But if another buyer also makes an offer, you could lose the chance of getting the house that's just right for your family.

Plan to sell your present house first, and then look for a new residence. You are in a better position as a buyer if you do not have contingencies, and a lot of money and time could be saved.

You can reduce the amount of time to buy a new house by taking these steps (see Figure 20–1):

1. *Investigate the new area.* Become thoroughly familiar with the condition of the market, average prices, and other important information.

2. *Pick your neighborhood.* Identify the part of town where you would like to live. Research transportation, schools, shopping, and other important features of the area.

3. *Find a broker.* Contact a real estate broker in your new city and ask for assistance comparing neighborhoods, housing prices, and the level of demand for residential property.

4. *Time your purchase.* Advise the new broker that you will be

FIGURE 20–1
Checklist: Speeding Up Your Move

✓ investigate the new area

✓ pick the neighborhood

✓ find a broker

✓ time your purchase

✓ contact a lender

---

needing a home in the near future. As soon as you have a buyer for your present home, get in touch with the new broker, plan to view several homes, and schedule buying trips to the new area.

5. *Contact a lender.* Fill out the application forms in advance. The lender can save a lot of time by requesting a credit check and evaluating you as a risk, before you find your new home. Then, when you are ready to make an offer, the lender will need only to appraise the house. The lender will already know whether you are creditworthy.

By planning ahead, you can eliminate many of the uncertainties of moving to a new area. The worst mistake you can make is deciding where you're going to move without first checking out its economy. Housing prices might be significantly higher, the demand much greater, and lending terms more restrictive than you expect. By gathering your information in advance, there will be no surprises.

Contingency offers put you at a disadvantage as a new buyer. As a seller, you would prefer a straight offer. Remember that other sellers will feel the same way, so avoid the problem with a little preparation and timing.

You can help speed up the selling process by preparing for your own closing. Know what to expect, and be sure to fulfill all of the escrow requirements promptly. The closing process is examined in the following chapter.

CHAPTER 21

CLOSING THE DEAL

Once you and a buyer agree on the price and other terms of the sale, the escrow process begins. Escrow is the transfer of documents and funds involved in the sale of property. The process will take between 30 and 60 days if neither the seller nor the buyer present any delays, and if there is no problem conveying (transferring) the title.

The buyer must submit money for the agreed-upon down payment and other fees; the seller for agreed-upon work to be performed as part of the contract. Arranging financing for the buyer, investigating the title, taking out a new homeowner's insurance policy, recording and transferring title, and a number of other steps must be completed before escrow can close.

THE ESCROW PROCESS

An escrow agent is appointed to hold money and handle all of the paperwork involved in your sale. This applies even when you work without a real estate broker. An escrow agent should always be involved in the transfer, to protect the interests of both the seller and the buyer. A professional escrow agent is aware of all the steps that must be taken in the complex selling process. For the relatively small fee charged, you and the buyer will both benefit by using an escrow agent.

When you sell through a real estate broker, the broker will probably recommend an escrow company. When you sell on your own, you will have to locate and appoint your own escrow agent. Ask your banker for recommendations. In some states, the escrow agent will also serve in the role of title company or agent. Look for an escrow company with the following points in mind:

1. *Fees*. Compare fees that various agents charge.
2. *Location*. Select an escrow agent whose office is nearby, so you won't have to drive out of your way to deliver documents.

3. *Experience*. Make sure the agent is qualified and experienced to manage the closing of your property.

In escrow, you must deliver the deed to your home, as stated in your sale contract. You might also be required to deposit money. For example, if part of your contract calls for repairing your property, you will either pay a contractor directly, or deposit money with the escrow agent, who will then schedule payments to a contractor.

The buyer deposits the down payment and other money for closing costs and, in return, receives the deed to your property when escrow closes.

The escrow agent is responsible for a wide range of actions and recordings, including:

1. *Instructions*. Both buyer and seller are given lists of documents and money to be delivered.
2. *Deed*. You deliver the deed to the escrow agent, so that it can be transferred to the buyer.
3. *Recordings*. The escrow agent records the transfer of title, and ensures that all existing mortgages and liens are either transferred or reconveyed.
4. *Title report*. A report is requested from the title company. This report is an investigation of the status of title to ensure that no secured debts are outstanding at the time title is transferred.
5. *Receipts*. The agent collects all money due from the buyer and the seller, and holds it until the close.
6. *Prorations*. Some expenses must be split between you and the buyer. For instance, a property tax bill is due soon after the sale is completed. A portion applies to the period you owned the house, and a portion to the new buyer. The escrow agent calculates the split and adjusts for it as of the closing date.
7. *Insurance*. The buyer will have to apply for homeowner's insurance, and perhaps default or mortgage insurance. In addition, upon completion of the title report, a title insurance policy will be issued.
8. *Payments*. After all the documents are completed, recorded, and transferred, and you and the buyer have complied with all terms of the sale, the escrow agent disburses money. Any lenders with outstanding mortgage balances are paid off, and then you receive your net proceeds.

Figure 21–1 shows these escrow transactions.

FIGURE 21–1
Escrow Transactions

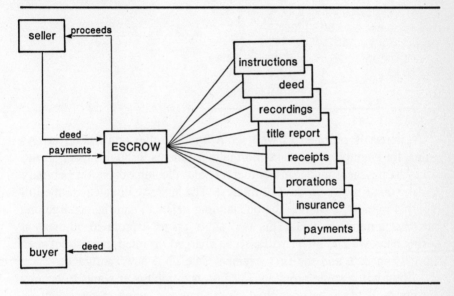

PRORATIONS

Proration, a division of money due or receivable between the two sides, takes place at the closing. Proration applies to property taxes, interest, rents, fire insurance, and—in the case of condominiums or cooperatives—association dues.

The split of any prorated expense occurs on the planned close of escrow date. The seller is responsible for liabilities up to that date; the buyer is responsible after that date (see Figure 21–2).

EXAMPLE:

Property taxes will be due on December 10 for the period starting January 1 and ending June 30. The total amount due will be $318. On December 1, you go into escrow with a buyer. The escrow agent pays the property tax bill from funds deposited by the buyer, and prorates the total expense. The planned closing date is February 16.

Using a 180-day calculation for the six months the property taxes cover, the proration is calculated as:

Seller: 46 days (January 1 to February 16)
Buyer: 134 days (February 17 to June 30)

Seller's share: 46/180 (25.6%)
Buyer's share: 134/180 (74.4%)

Seller's liability: 25.6% x $318 = $ 81.41
Buyer's liability: 74.4% x $318 = $236.59

Total = $318.00

Interest is prorated as well, both for the seller and the buyer. As seller, for example, you make mortgage payments through January, with your last payment made on February 1. But closing occurs on February 16, so you still owe 15 days of interest. The lender will calculate the full month's interest, based on the outstanding balance, and then charge one half that amount to you. This will show up as a prorated adjustment during escrow. The buyer will also be charged prorated interest between the closing date and the first payment date on a new mortgage.

Rent will also be prorated. For instance, the buyer wants to occupy the house 10 days before actual close, and you agree to move out on February 6. As a closing adjustment, the escrow agent will calculate 10 days of rent (based on the agreement you make with the buyer) and credit you with that amount. The buyer is charged as part of the closing adjustments.

Another form of rent proration applies when the house is occupied by a tenant. For example, rent was paid to you for the full month of February. The new owner plans to continue the lease under its present terms, and is entitled to 13 days of rent income (February 16 to 28).

FIGURE 21–2
Prorations

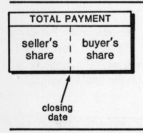

You will receive a prorated refund for part of homeowner's insurance paid for a full year. If you are selling a condo or co-op, the monthly assessment for common area maintenance will be split between you and the buyer as of the closing date.

THE CLOSING STATEMENT

As the seller, you will be responsible for several forms of payment from proceeds of the sale. These include:

Prorations

Payments to lenders of all existing loans, including principal and interest

Payments of outstanding liens on the property

Reconveyance, notary, and recording fees

Transfer tax

Real estate agent's commission

Escrow agent's fee

Attorney fees

Payments for agreed upon repair work

The balance you receive consists of the sales price minus these closing costs. The buyer is also responsible for a variety of payments, including prorations, homeowner's insurance, title search and title insurance premiums, inspection fees, notary fees, recording fees, transfer tax, points on a new loan, loan origination fees, and a credit report. In addition, the buyer must deposit the required down payment.

The seller and the buyer will receive a preliminary and a final closing statement. Both are necessary for a number of reasons. The preliminary statement estimates the actual expenses, and enables the seller and buyer to fulfill escrow requirements. Just prior to the close, the title company will perform a final check of the title to ensure that no new liens have been placed on the property. They then issue their final title report. The escrow agent then prepares the final closing statement and disburses funds.

EXAMPLE:

You sell your home for $95,000. You have the following closing adjustments:

$	81.41	prorated property taxes
	22.00	reconveyance fee
	2.00	notary fee
	95.00	transfer tax
	6.00	recording fee
	5,700.00	real estate commission
	48,315.00	principal on your mortgage
	140.92	interest (prorated from Feb. 1)

These adjustments total $54,362.33. Subtracted from the sales price, it leaves $40,637.67. Upon close of escrow, you will be issued a check in this amount. A summary of these transactions is shown in Figure 21–3.

Money is disbursed in escrow depending on a number of factors, such as the form of ownership registration for your home, whether or not you are taking back a loan for the buyer, and the exact terms of your sale

FIGURE 21–3

---

closing summary

	DEBITS	CREDITS
sale price		95,000.00
prorated taxes 1–1 to 2–16	81.41	
reconveyance fee	22.00	
notary fee	2.00	
transfer tax	95.00	
recording fee	6.00	
commission, 6%	5,700.00	
first mortgage:		
principal	48,315.00	
interest	140.92	
check to seller	40,637.67	
total	95,000.00	95,000.00

contract. The complexities of contracts, deeds, title, financing, and other issues of selling your home can require a lot of outside advice. Your real estate broker, banker, escrow agent, and attorney can provide guidance throughout the selling and escrow process.

Section 3 explores tax considerations after the sale, and looks ahead to your transition from seller to buyer.

SECTION 3

AFTER THE SALE

CHAPTER 22

DEFERRING YOUR PROFITS

The federal tax laws favor you as a seller. All of the profits from your home can be deferred, often indefinitely, as long as you buy a new house that costs more than the sales price of your present house.

This can make a big difference. You have owned your house for 15 years, for instance, and real estate values have changed dramatically. Your house cost you $40,000, but you sell it for $95,000. If you're taxed on that $55,000 profit, you'll lose about $15,000 of the total profit to federal taxes.

You do not escape taxes on your profit, you merely defer them. But if you invest in a new home, it's likely that you can defer profits for many years to come.

Profits will be taxed only when you sell a home and do not buy a new one. For example, upon retirement, you sell your house and become a renter. You will then be taxed for the profits you earned—not only on the sale of the final house, but on the deferred profits from other houses you owned in the past as well. As you'll see in Chapter 26, there is yet another benefit in the tax law that enables you to escape being taxed on those profits, too.

HOW DEFERRAL WORKS

Deferral of profits means that the gain will be taxed in some future year, rather than during the year they are earned. So for tax purposes, the "basis" (cost plus or minus adjustments) of your new home is reduced by the amount of deferred profit.

EXAMPLE:

You sell your present home for $95,000. Closing costs are $5,825, so the net sale price is $89,175. The house originally cost you $39,100 many years ago. Adding closing costs of $1,300, your adjusted purchase price is $40,300. The profit on your sale is $48,875.

As long as you buy a new house within two years of the sale date, and as long as the purchase price is higher than the adjusted sale price ($89,175), all profits are deferred. Assume you purchase a new home for $105,000. Closing costs are $3,600, so the adjusted purchase price is $108,600. Subtracting the deferred profits of $48,875, your tax basis in the new home is only $59,725. When you later sell the house, the profit will be computed as the difference between the sale price and $59,725 (see Figure 22–1).

This rule applies only if you trade up; that is, buy a house that costs more than the adjusted sale price of your previous home. By trading up, you improve your lifestyle, move to a better neighborhood, or increase your living space. At the same time, you increase the value of your real estate investment, while deferring federal taxes.

The deferral rule has several limitations. These are:

1. *Two-year restriction.* You cannot trade up more than once in each two-year period.

FIGURE 22–1

	adjusted basis	
OLD HOUSE		
sale price	$95,000	
less: closing costs	−5,825	
adjusted sale price		$89,175
purchase price	$39,000	
plus: closing costs	1,300	
adjusted purchase price		$40,300
profit		$48,875
NEW HOUSE		
purchase price	$105,000	
plus: closing costs	3,600	
adjusted purchase price		$108,600
less: deferred profit		−48,875
adjusted basis		$ 59,725

EXAMPLE:

You sell your present house and defer the gain. But 18 months later, you sell your new house and earn another profit. You cannot defer your gains on the second transaction, since it occurred within two years.

2. *Some uses do not qualify.* Deferral excludes rentals and home office use. You cannot defer profits on any portion of your house used for business or rented out to someone else.

EXAMPLE:

You use 14 percent of your floor space as an office in the home, and claim tax deductions for it. Upon sale, 14 percent of your total gain will be taxed; the remainder qualifies for deferral.

EXAMPLE:

You rent out one third of your home to a tenant. Upon sale, one third of your total profit will be taxed in the year of sale.

3. *Principal residences only.* Both homes must be your principal residences. If you also own rental or vacation properties, the deferral rules do not apply. And you can have only one principal residence. By the definition of the federal tax code, a principal residence is one that you lived in for no less than three of the past five years.

EXAMPLE:

You own two homes—a residence and a rental property. When you sell the rental house, you make a profit of $32,000. Even though you buy another rental house within two years, none of the profit can be deferred.

EXAMPLE:

You own two homes and want to sell them both at the same time. You lived in one for 38 months and the other for 22 months. The first one is considered your principal residence, regardless of which house you actually occupied as a principal residence during the time immediately before the sale. The deferral rules can be applied only to profits on that house. Profits on the other are taxed in the year of sale.

4. *Two years to occupy.* You must physically occupy your new house within two years from the date of sale of your old house. To qualify for deferral, you must move within 24 months—either before or after the sale date.

EXAMPLE:

You decide to have a custom house built, so you purchase land and hire a contractor. The project takes eight months to complete; selling your present house takes another six months. The total, 14 months, is within the two-year limit. You can defer the profit on your first house. Even though you bought and paid for your new house before selling your old one, the deferral rules apply—as long as you move within two years before or after the sale date.

EXAMPLE:

You sell your present house and move to an apartment. But 18 months later, you decide you'd rather own another home. So you make an offer, and the sale is complete 60 days later. You are still within the two-year limit, and qualify for deferral. Again, you must actually close the transaction and occupy your new home within two years.

5. *Must trade up for 100 percent.* To defer all profits, the purchase price of your new home must exceed the sale price of your old home. When it's less, the difference is taxable in the year of sale.

EXAMPLE:

The adjusted sales price of your old home is $89,175. The profit is $48,875. You purchase a new home, paying an adjusted price of $85,000. The difference between the sale and purchase price is $4,175, and is taxable in the current year. The balance of profit, $44,700, is deferred. (See Figure 22–2.)

6. *No loss deductions.* Although you will eventually be taxed on all gains from selling your home, you cannot claim a tax deduction for a loss. However, you can claim losses for investment property.

FIGURE 22–2

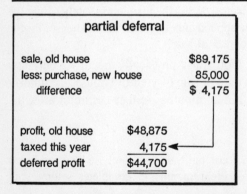

EXAMPLE:

The adjusted purchase price on your home is $108,600. Two years later, you move to another town, and sell your home for an adjusted sale price of $102,000. Your loss of $6,600 is not deductible.

EXAMPLE:

You purchase a second home, rent it out for five years, and then sell it. On an adjusted basis, you lose money. This is deductible as an investment loss, subject to limits on deductibility of losses in any one year.

Figure 22–3 summarizes these limitations on deferrals of taxes.

MULTIPLE DEFERRALS

Within the limits of the deferral rule, you can buy and sell several homes over your lifetime, and never be taxed on any of the profit. So long as the adjusted purchase price of your new home exceeds the adjusted sales price of your old home, and the transaction does not exceed the two-year limit, deferral continues on from one house to another.

EXAMPLE:

Over many years, you buy and sell three homes before you retire. Upon retirement, you buy one final home to live in. Your first home cost $39,000 and the last one is valued at $150,000. None of your profits are taxable:

FIGURE 22–3
Deferral Limitations

1. Two–year restriction
2. Some uses do not qualify
3. Principal residences only
4. Two years to occupy
5. Must trade up for 100%
6. No loss deductions

	House # 1	House # 2	House # 3	House # 4
Purchase price	$39,000	$105,000	$125,000	$150,000
Closing costs	1,300	3,600	4,100	5,200
Deferred profit	0	− 48,875	− 57,075	− 52,975
Adjusted basis	$40,300	$ 59,725	$ 72,025	$102,225
Sale price	$95,000	$125,000	$134,000	
Closing costs	− 5,825	− 8,200	− 9,000	
Adjusted sale	$89,175	$116,800	$125,000	
Profit	$48,875	$ 57,075	$ 52,975	

Remember that you have two years to buy a new home, in order to qualify for tax deferral. So if you sell a house, become a renter, and then decide later to buy a house, the tax advantages can still apply. However, this raises a question of reporting taxes. If you are not sure whether you will buy another house, do you report and pay taxes on the gain now? Or, do you wait and see? If you report the gain and later buy another house, you will have to amend your previous tax return and apply for a refund.

The rules for tax deferral and reporting are complex. In most instances, deferral is not a choice. If you buy or build another home, you must defer profits. You cannot choose to pay taxes now.

A professional tax adviser should always be consulted when you report profits—or defer them—following the sale of your principal residence. And the decision about whether or not to sell, the timing of that decision, and the amount of profit you realize, should be guided by your personal needs and priorities, not solely by tax advantages.

CHAPTER 23

TAXES ON YOUR PROFITS

You are required to report the sale of your house to the Internal Revenue Service, as part of your annual tax return. You must report even when you defer profits, or when you have a loss. The deferral of profits is not a choice. If you buy or build another home within two years from the date of sale, profits are automatically deferred. This chapter explains how to complete the required tax forms and schedules.

REPORTING THE SALE

When you sell your home, Form 2119 must be attached to your tax return. The form is available from any Internal Revenue Service (IRS) office. You should also pick up *Publication 523, Tax Information on Selling Your Home,* a free booklet that explains the rules for home sellers in detail.

Form 2119 (Figure 23–1) serves several purposes. It can be used for information only. In the event you do not have a profit, or if profits are deferred, the form shows the details of the transaction. It is always filed in the year of the sale. When there is a taxable profit (either because you do not buy another house, or because you must report a portion of your gain), Form 2119 provides the details supporting the entry you make elsewhere on the tax return.

What if you don't know whether or not you will buy another home within two years? In that case, you will file two Form 2119s. The first is filed for the year of the sale. Only lines 1 and 2 are completed, and no gain is reported for that year. If you do not buy another house within the two-year limit, you must file an amended tax return for the year of sale, using Form 1040-X and another Form 2119. Interest will be charged on the amount of tax owed, from the original due date of the tax return to the date the amended return is filed and taxes are paid.

Some people believe at the time they sell that they will not buy

FIGURE 23–1

Form **2119**	**Sale or Exchange of Principal Residence**	OMB No. 1545-0072
Department of the Treasury Internal Revenue Service (O)	▶ See instructions on back. ▶ Attach to Form 1040 for year of sale (see instruction B).	**1987** Attachment Sequence No. **22**
Name(s) as shown on Form 1040.		Your social security number

Do not include expenses that you deduct as moving expenses.

1 a Date former residence sold ▶

   b Enter the face amount of any mortgage, note (for example, second trust), or other financial instrument on which you will receive periodic payments of principal or interest from this sale ▶

		Yes	No
2 a	If you bought or built a new residence, enter date you occupied it; otherwise enter "None" ▶		
b	Are any rooms in either residence rented out or used for business for which a deduction is allowed? . . . . (If "Yes," see instructions.)		
3 a	Were you 55 or over on date of sale?		
b	Was your spouse 55 or over on date of sale? . . . . If you answered "No" to 3a and 3b, do not complete 3c through 3f and Part II.		
c	Did the person who answered "Yes" to 3a or 3b own and use the property sold as his or her principal residence for a total of at least 3 years (except for short absences) of the 5-year period before the sale?		
d	If you answered "Yes" to 3c, do you elect to take the once in a lifetime exclusion of the gain on the sale?		
e	At time of sale, was the residence owned by: ☐ you, ☐ your spouse, ☐ both of you?		
f	Social security number of spouse, at time of sale, if different from number on Form 1040 ▶ (Enter "None" if you were not married at time of sale.)		

Part I   Computation of Gain

4	Selling price of residence (Do not include personal property items.)	**4**	
5	Expense of sale (Include sales commissions, advertising, legal, etc.)	**5**	
6	Subtract line 5 from line 4. This is the amount realized · . ·	**6**	
7	Basis of residence sold	**7**	
8	Gain on sale (subtract line 7 from line 6). If zero or less, enter zero and do not complete the rest of form. Enter the gain from this line on Schedule D, line 3 or 10,* unless you bought another principal residence or checked "Yes" to 3d. Then continue with this form	**8**	
	If you haven't replaced your residence, do you plan to do so within the replacement period? . . . . ☐ Yes ☐ No (If "Yes" see instruction B.)		

Part II   Age 55 or Over One-Time Exclusion

Complete this part only if you checked "yes" to 3(d) to elect the once in a lifetime exclusion; otherwise, skip to Part III.

9	Enter the smaller of line 8 or $125,000 ($62,500, if married filing separate return)	**9**	
10	Gain (subtract line 9 from line 8). If zero, do not complete rest of form. Enter the gain from this line on Schedule D, line 10,* unless you bought another principal residence. Then continue with this form . .	**10**	

Part III   Gain To Be Postponed and Adjusted Basis of New Residence

Complete this part if you bought another principal residence.

11	Fixing-up expenses (see instructions for time limits)	**11**	
12	Adjusted sales price (subtract line 11 from line 6)	**12**	
13	Cost of new residence	**13**	
14	Gain taxable this year (subtract line 13 plus line 9 (if applicable) from line 12). If result is zero or less, enter zero. Do not enter more than line 8 or line 10 (if applicable). Enter the gain from this line on Schedule D, line 3 or 10*	**14**	
15	Gain to be postponed (Subtract line 14 from line 8. However, if Part II applies, subtract line 14 from line 10.) . . . . · · . . .	**15**	
16	Adjusted basis of new residence (subtract line 15 from line 13)	**16**	

*****Caution:** If you completed Form 6252 for the residence in 1a, do not enter your taxable gain from Form 2119 on Schedule D.

For Paperwork Reduction Act Notice, see back of form.   Form **2119** (1987) another home, and decide to pay the taxes on their profit when the original tax return is filed. But they subsequently do buy another home. In this case, an amended return is also filed, with a corrected Form 2119. A refund is then paid to them.

Most people know they will buy another home, and defer all or part of their gain. If it occurs within a single year, Form 2119 can be filed once, and all information can be provided on the form.

Form 2119 shows the computation of gains or losses when you replace one home with another. You are allowed to reduce your profits for fixing-up expenses, which are explained in Chapter 25. You also report the expenses of the sale, such as real estate commissions and other closing costs.

On line 7 of the form, the basis of residence is reported. If you are selling your first home, basis is the original cost (adjusted for closing costs), plus any additions made to your house. You also deduct any casualty losses suffered, as well as previously claimed energy credits. For information on computing your basis, see Chapter 24. Also ask the IRS for a free copy of *Publication 551, Basis of Assets*.

If this is not your first house, you probably deferred gains from a previously sold property. In this case, basis will be reduced to the extent of gains you deferred in the past.

EXAMPLE:

You sold your first home for $87,000 and earned a profit (after adjustments) of $20,000. Your current home was bought for $90,000. The basis is $70,000:

Cost of current home	90,000
Less deferred gain	− 20,000
Adjusted basis	$70,000

The profit being reported this year shows up on line 8 or 14 (if a portion of the gain is taxable). Even if you buy another house, you might have to pay tax on a portion of your gain.

EXAMPLE:

You sell your current house for $95,000 (adjusted price) and buy another for $92,000. You will be taxed on the difference of $3,000:

Sale price	95,000
Purchase price, new home	− 92,000
Gain taxed this year	$ 3,000

The balance of your gain will be deferred, as explained in Chapter 22.

SUMMARIZING THE GAIN

Any taxable gain this year is also reported on Schedule D, Capital Gains and Losses. Figure 23–2 shows the first page of Schedule D. You will report gains under one of two parts on this form. Part I is for short-term capital gains, and is used if you owned your house for six months or less. Line 3 is completed in this situation. Part II is used if you owned your home more than six months. Line 10 is completed.

The Tax Reform Act of 1986 changed the rules for taxes on capital gains. Before 1987, short-term gains were fully taxable and a portion of long-term gains was excluded from tax. Beginning in 1987, there is no difference. All capital gains are subject to the same tax rates as other income.

The distinction between short- and long-term gains has been left intact in the new tax law. Schedule D is the same as before the change, on the chance that in future years, the favorable rates on long-term gains might be reinstated.

The amount of gain you report on the front of Schedule D is also shown on the reverse side, under Part III, Summary. The second page of Schedule D is shown in Figure 23–3. The gain from this schedule is also transferred to the front page of Form 1040. It is added to your other income, for the purpose of figuring out the total amount of tax owed for the year.

Remember that even if you have no gain to report, you must still file Form 2119 as part of your tax return, in the year your sale is completed. If you do have a taxable gain, you show it in Form 2119, then transfer the total to Schedule D, then to Form 1040 (see Figure 23–4).

The federal tax rules have changed significantly in recent years. Between 1980 and 1986, there was an average of one major new tax bill each year. You should expect further changes in the future, and should

FIGURE 23–2

SCHEDULE D (Form 1040) Department of the Treasury Internal Revenue Service (O)	**Capital Gains and Losses and Reconciliation of Forms 1099-B** ▶ Attach to Form 1040. ▶ See Instructions for Schedule D (Form 1040). For Paperwork Reduction Act Notice, see Form 1040 Instructions.	OMB No. 1545-0074 **1987** Attachment Sequence No. **12**

Name(s) as shown on Form 1040 | Your social security number

1 Report here, the total sales of stocks, bonds, etc., reported for 1987 by your broker to you on Form(s) 1099-B or an equivalent substitute statement(s). If this amount differs from the total of lines 2b and 9b, column (d), attach a statement explaining the difference. See the Instructions for line 1 for examples. Do not include real estate transactions reported to you on a Form 1099-B on line 1, 2a, or 9a **1**

Part I Short-term Capital Gains and Losses—Assets Held Six Months or Less

(a) Description of property (Example, 100 shares 7% preferred of "Z" Co.)	(b) Date acquired (Mo., day, yr.)	(c) Date sold (Mo., day, yr.)	(d) Sales price (see Instructions)	(e) Cost or other basis (see Instructions)	(f) LOSS If (e) is more than (d), subtract (d) from (e)	(g) GAIN If (d) is more than (e), subtract (e) from (d)
2a Form 1099-B Transactions (Sales of Stocks, Bonds, etc.): (Do not report real estate transactions here. See the instructions for lines 2a and 9a.)						

2b Total (add column (d)) . . . . ▶

2c Other Transactions:

3 Short-term gain from sale or exchange of a principal residence from Form 2119, lines 8 or 14   **3**
4 Short-term gain from installment sales from Form 6252, lines 23 or 31 . . .   **4**
5 Net short-term gain or (loss) from partnerships, S corporations, and fiduciaries .   **5**
6 Short-term capital loss carryover **6**
7 Add all of the transactions on lines 2a and 2c and lines 3 through 6 in columns (f) and (g) . . .   **7** (   )
8 Net short-term gain or (loss), combine columns (f) and (g) of line 7 . . . .   **8**

Part II Long-term Capital Gains and Losses—Assets Held More Than Six Months

9a Form 1099-B Transactions (Sales of Stocks, Bonds, etc.): (Do not report real estate transactions here. See the instructions for lines 2a and 9a.)						

9b Total (add column (d)) . . . . ▶

9c Other Transactions:

10 Long-term gain from sale or exchange of a principal residence from Form 2119, lines 8, 10, or 14   **10**
11 Long-term gain from installment sales from Form 6252, lines 23 or 31 . . . .   **11**
12 Net long-term gain or (loss) from partnerships, S corporations, and fiduciaries . .   **12**
13 Capital gain distributions **13**
14 Enter gain from Form 4797, line 7 or 9 . . . .   **14**
15 Long-term capital loss carryover **15**
16 Add all of the transactions on lines 9a and 9c and lines 10 through 15 in columns (f) and (g) . . .   **16** (   )
17 Net long-term gain or (loss), combine columns (f) and (g) of line 16 . . . .   **17**

Schedule D (Form 1040) 1987

FIGURE 23–3

Schedule D (Form 1040) 1987   Attachment Sequence No. **12**   Page **2**

Name(s) as shown on Form 1040. (Do not enter name and social security number if shown on other side.)   **Your social security number**

Part III   **Summary of Parts I and II**

18	Combine lines 8 and 17, and enter the net gain or (loss) here. If result is a gain, also enter the gain on Form 1040, line 14	18
	Note: If lines 17 and 18 are net gains and your taxable income is taxed over the 28% tax rate, see Part IV below. You may be able to reduce your tax if you qualify for the alternative tax computation.	
19	If line 18 is a loss, enter here and as a loss on Form 1040, line 14, the **smaller** of:	
a	The amount on line 18; **or b** $3,000 ($1,500 if married filing a separate return)	19

Part IV   **Alternative Tax Computation**
First complete Form 1040 through line 36.

Use Part IV if both lines 17 and 18 show net gains, AND:

You checked filing status box:	AND	Form 1040, line 36 is over:	You checked filing status box:	AND	Form 1040, line 36 is over:
1		$27,000	3		$22,500
2 or 5		45,000	4		38,000

20	Enter amount from Form 1040, line 36	20
21	Enter the smaller of the gain on line 17 or the gain on line 18	21
22	Subtract line 21 from 20 and enter the result	22
23	Enter: **a** $16,800 if you checked filing status box 1; **b** $28,000 if you checked filing status box 2 or 5; **c** $14,000 if you checked filing status box 3; **or d** $23,000 if you checked filing status box 4	23
24	Enter the **greater** of line 22 or line 23	24
25	Subtract line 24 from iine 20	25
26	Figure the amount of tax on line 24. Use the Tax Table or Tax Rate Schedules, whichever applies . . .	26
27	Multiply line 25 by 28% (.28) and enter the result	27
28	Add lines 26 and 27. Enter the result here and on Form 1040, line 37 and check the box for Schedule D	28

Part V   **Computation of Capital Loss Carryovers From 1987 to 1988**
(Complete this part if the loss on line 18 is more than the loss on line 19.)

29	Enter the loss shown on line 8; if none, enter zero and skip lines 30 through 33.	29
30	Enter gain shown on line 17. If that line is blank or shows a loss, enter zero	30
31	Subtract line 30 from line 29	31
32	Enter the smaller of line 19 or 31	32
33	Subtract line 32 from line 31. This is your **short-term capital loss carryover from 1987 to 1988** . .	33
34	Enter loss from line 17; if none, enter zero and skip lines 35 through 38	34
35	Enter gain shown on line 8. If that line is blank or shows a loss, enter zero	35
36	Subtract line 35 from line 34	36
37	Subtract line 32 from line 19. (**Note:** If you skipped lines 30 through 33, enter the amount from line 19.)	37
38	Subtract line 37 from line 36. This is your **long-term capital loss carryover from 1987 to 1988** . . .	38

Part VI   **Complete This Part Only If You Elect Out of the Installment Method and Report a Note or Other Obligation at Less Than Full Face Value**

39	Check here if you elect out of the installment method . . . . ▶ ☐
40	Enter the face amount of the note or other obligation . . . . ▶ ....
41	Enter the percentage of valuation of the note or other obligation . . . . . . ▶

Part VII   **Reconciliation of Forms 1099-B for Bartering Transactions**
Complete this part if you received one or more Form(s) 1099-B or an equivalent substitute statement(s) reporting bartering income.

Amount of bartering income from Form 1099-B or equivalent statement reported on form or schedule

42	Form 1040, line 21	42
43	Schedule C (Form 1040)	43
44	Schedule D (Form 1040)	44
45	Schedule E (Form 1040)	45
46	Schedule F (Form 1040)	46
47	Other (identify) (if not taxable, indicate reason—attach additional sheets if necessary) ▶	47
48	Total (add lines 42 through 47)	48

Note: The amount on line 48 should be the same as the total bartering income on all Forms 1099-B or equivalent statements received.

☆ U.S. GOVERNMENT PRINTING OFFICE:1987-183-097/87-0367773

FIGURE 23–4
Reporting the Gain

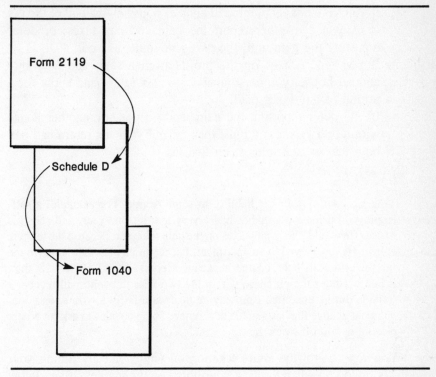

always consult with a tax expert in any year you sell or buy a home. If you must file an amended return, you should also seek help from a tax professional.

THE EFFECT OF TAX

Paying tax on all or part of the gain you make from selling your home will reduce the actual money you make. The amount of additional tax depends on your tax bracket, and to compute the actual effect, you should figure out your taxes with and without the sale of your house.

Once you sell your home, you have no choice about the timing of reporting your gain. The following rules must be observed:

1. You cannot elect to be taxed on a gain this year if you do buy another house. The gain must be deferred.
2. If you have not yet purchased another house by the end of the tax year, you can either report the gain and pay taxes; or defer reporting the gain until the two-year limit runs out.
3. If you report taxes on the profits from a sale, and later buy another house, you must amend your tax return and apply for a refund of any taxes paid.
4. If you defer reporting the gain, and do not buy another house within two years, you must then amend your tax return and pay both the tax and interest on that tax.

EXAMPLE:

You can control your tax liability to some degree. For example, a self-employed business owner has had a very low income year, and sells his house. He would like to pay taxes on the gain this year, because the tax rate is low. He has moved to an apartment, but might buy another house in the future. Two years later, he does make an offer on a house. He realizes that, if he concludes the purchase within the two-year limit, he will receive a refund. But he benefited from paying taxes at a fairly low rate, and does not want change the basis in his new home. So he decides to ask for a later closing date on his new house.

You can control the entire taxation on your home by timing your sale. It's up to you when to place your home on the market. If you know you will not buy another house, you should figure out how the gain will affect this year's tax liability.

EXAMPLE:

A family plans to sell its house this year. The children have grown up and left home, and the parents have decided to move to a small apartment. But their income is in the top tax bracket. Next year, when both father and mother plan to retire, income will be much lower. By putting off the sale a few months, they can shift the gain to the following year, and pay taxes at a lower rate.

Up to $125,000 of taxable gain can be excluded from taxes if you and your spouse are 55 or older, due to a one-time exclusion everyone is allowed. See Chapter 26 for details.

Tax considerations should always be understood before a sale is made. Get professional advice in advance. However, you should not time your move only for tax reasons. Sell your house when you want or need to sell it. Don't allow a tax motive solely to change your plans. In some cases, though, delaying your decision by a few months can save you a lot of money. If a delay will make little or no difference to you, do consider one for tax purposes.

EXAMPLE:

Your original reason for wanting to move is to buy a smaller apartment or house. You no longer need a large house, and the monthly cost of utilities and maintenance is too high. If you delay selling a full year just for tax reasons, you might save a few thousand dollars in taxes. But you'll spend that much in too-high expenses by keeping your home that extra time.

The following chapter explains how the basis in your home is computed, and how deferred gains might affect future profits and taxes.

CHAPTER 24

FIGURING YOUR
ADJUSTED BASIS

There are a number of possible adjustments you will have to compute to accurately arrive at your cost basis. On the additions side are closing costs paid at the time of purchase, and the cost of additions to your house. On the reductions side is any depreciation claimed, either for rental of all or part of your house, or for expenses in connection with an office in your home.

THE PURPOSE OF ADJUSTMENTS

Why must you compute the adjusted basis? Two major reasons are to satisfy the requirements of tax law, and to figure out how much your home has appreciated over the period of time you owned it. In the latter case, the formula is somewhat different than the strictly tax-based computation.

For tax purposes, you must either pay tax on the profit from your sale, or defer all or part of that profit (when you buy or build another home within two years from the date of sale). In either case, you will need to know your adjusted basis.

A tax liability is figured out by subtracting the adjusted cost basis of your home from its net realized price. The "realized price" is the actual price you receive, less commissions, other closing costs, and any fixing-up expenses done in anticipation of a sale. These are explained in Chapter 25.

Adjusted basis, as shown in Figure 24–1, is the first half of this formula. The taxable profit consists of the realized price, less the adjusted basis.

If you used part of your home for business, or as investment property, you must reduce your basis for the amount of depreciation you claimed on your tax returns.

Depreciation is figured on the cost of the building and any improvements made. It's important to keep in mind that it's the cost—not current market value—that serves as the base for depreciation.

EXAMPLE:

> You bought your home for $35,000 many years ago. At the time, land was worth approximately $10,000 and the building was worth $25,000. Today, the total property is valued at about $100,000. If you claim depreciation, it must be based on your cost, or $25,000. If you added an extra room that cost $15,000, then your depreciation base is increased to $40,000.

Another restriction applies. You can depreciate only that portion of your home that was actually rented out or used for business.

EXAMPLE:

> You bought your home for $35,000 and spent another $1,250 on closing costs. You later added a room costing $15,000. Estimating the value of land at $10,000 (at the time of purchase), your depreciable base is $41,250. You used one room exclusively for business. The room measures out to 15 percent of your total useable floor space. Only 15 percent of your building's cost is subject to depreciation.

Depreciation on residential property is allowed over 27.5 years as of 1988, and only on the straight-line basis, which means you can claim the same amount every year. So if your total floor space is 4,000 feet and you use a 600-foot room as a home office, you can claim only 15 percent of the allowable depreciation (see Figure 24–2).

Cost basis	$41,250
Depreciation (27.5 years)	$ 1,500
15% limitation	$ 225

FIGURE 24–1
Adjusted Basis

original cost
plus: additions
less: reductions
= adjusted basis

FIGURE 24–2
Depreciation

original purchase price	$35,000
plus: closing costs	1,250
room addition	15,000
total cost basis	$51,250
less: cost of land	10,000
building's cost basis	$41,250
yearly depreciation	$ 1,500
15%	$ 225

HOME OFFICE LIMITATIONS

The potential deduction for depreciation when you have an office at home is severely limited, because the term for claiming depreciation is long— 27.5 years—and you can deduct only the portion that actually applies to business.

Many people who work at home do not even claim depreciation, for several reasons:

1. For the limited amount of tax benefit, claiming home office expenses increases the chance of being audited. Self-employed people are specifically asked on Schedule C of their tax returns, whether they are claiming expenses for an office in the home.

2. Qualifying for a home office deduction is not easy. Most people, even those who work at home full time, will have difficulty meeting all of the tests of the tax law.

3. Claiming depreciation disallows the deferral of profits upon sale of the home. So if you anticipate putting your home on the market, you will receive a limited tax benefit; when you sell, you will be taxed on the profits from that portion of your home used as an office.

To take a depreciation deduction, you must use a portion of your home exclusively and regularly for business. It must be your principal place of business, in most cases. If you are employed by someone else, you cannot claim a deduction if the home office is merely for the convenience of your employer. It must virtually be a condition of employment that you maintain a home office.

Even full-time self-employed people will not always be able to qualify. A room must be *exclusively* and *regularly* used for business purposes. So if you work in a room where you also store personal belongings, have a television set, or use—even occasionally—for nonbusiness reasons, you are not entitled to a deduction. If you work at home and maintain an office, you should call or write the IRS to obtain a free copy of *Publication 587, Business Use of Your Home.*

If you rent out a portion of your home, you are allowed to claim depreciation only for that portion rented out (usually figured on a square-foot basis), and only for the period of time you collected rent.

EXAMPLE:

You rented out a room for six months last year. The area of that room equals approximately 12 percent of your total living space. You are entitled to depreciation on only 6 percent of your home's adjusted basis. Although the room is equal to 12 percent of the total, it was rented out only for six months, or half of the year.

To compute your basis, you begin with the adjusted purchase price, add any additions, and subtract all depreciation claimed.

EXAMPLE:

Your home cost $35,000 plus $1,250 in closing costs. You spent $15,000 to add a room, and claimed a total of $675 of depreciation over three years (at $225 per year). Your adjusted basis is $50,575 (original cost plus closing costs, plus the room addition, and minus depreciation). See Figure 24–3.

FIGURE 24–3
Computing Adjustments

original purchase price	$35,000
plus: closing costs	1,250
adjusted purchase price	$36,250
plus: room addition	15,000
total cost basis	$51,250
less: depreciation	675
adjusted basis	$50,575

For the purpose of basis, some closing costs are added; others are not. The following rules apply:

1. If the closing cost is a prorated tax or interest charge, it is deductible in the year of purchase, but is not added to the basis.
2. If part of your closing costs includes a year's premium for homeowner's insurance, it is not deductible, and also is not added to your basis because it's an ongoing expense of owning your home.
3. Title insurance, transfer and recording fees, inspections, and other costs are added to your basis.

INVESTMENT BASIS

The basis for tax purposes does not recognize any ongoing expenses, such as homeowner's insurance, maintenance, property taxes, or interest on your mortgage. For the purpose of figuring out the actual investment value of your property, however, the adjusted basis should be expanded. For accuracy, you should figure the cost of owning your home after taxes. So expenses like mortgage interest and property taxes should be discounted to allow for the tax advantages they produced. These can be significant sums.

EXAMPLE:

Paying on an $80,000 mortgage at 10 percent interest (30-year term), your first year's payments add up to $8,425, of which about $7,980 is interest. If your combined federal and state tax rates equal 33 percent, paying interest reduces your taxes by $2,633 during the first year.

Compute your tax savings as follows. Reduce your itemized deductions by the amount of interest and property taxes you claimed, then compute what your tax liability would have been. Subtract this from the actual taxes you paid. The balance is the amount you saved. Be sure to include both interest and property taxes, and figure the savings on both federal and state taxes, if applicable. Next, add in the annual cost of homeowner's insurance, routine maintenance, and utilities. Subtract the estimated cost of insurance and utilities you would have paid if you rented an apartment.

EXAMPLE:

Your adjusted basis for tax purposes is $50,575. You figure out the aftertax cost of mortgage interest, property taxes, maintenance, and utilities over the period you owned your home, and it adds up to $32,000. Most of this is for interest. After owning your home for five years (assuming a 30-year loan at 10 percent interest), you will have paid off only 3.43 percent of principal. The rest of your payments all went to interest. So if your mortgage was for $80,000, five years of payments add up to $42,125. Of that, only $2,741 went to reduction of principal.

On an investment basis:

Adjusted basis (for tax purposes)	$50,575
Plus: expenses of owning the home	32,000
Investment basis	$82,575

If your adjusted sale price is lower than the investment basis, you actually have lost money on the transaction. In the past—notably before 1982—real estate could increase in value from $35,000 to $85,000 or more. But by the mid-1980s, that level of growth was less likely.

To demonstrate how investment return works, assume you sell your home for $100,000 (adjusted basis after commissions and other closing costs). Your profit is $17,425 over a five-year period, or 21.1 percent ($17,425 divided by the investment basis of $82,575). On average, that's 4.22 percent per year. Figuring the investment basis requires a certain amount of estimating, and it is not a completely accurate return, for a number of reasons. For example, it assumes that the cost of renting would have been unchanging, which is not accurate. It also assumes an average cost of utilities you would have paid as a renter. It also fails to consider the improvement in your lifestyle and personal comfort as a result of owning your own home.

Considering that you don't actually "take profits" from selling your home, you might think of the investment basis as only a theory. You will probably reinvest your proceeds in a new home, so any equity you've built up is converted rather than realized. In comparison, someone who buys stock and then sells it at a profit does realize—or take—that profit and pay taxes on it.

The next chapter discusses how fixing-up expenses alter the adjusted sale price of your home, and how moving expenses are treated for tax purposes.

CHAPTER 25

PREPARATION COSTS

Fixing-up expenses—money spent in anticipation of a sale—reduce the tax basis of your home. Just as the purchase price is adjusted, the sales price is not just the amount you receive. In most instances, the tax basis (used to figure any taxable gains in the year of sale) consists of the sales price, less commissions and closing costs, and less any fixing-up expenses.

HOW THE ADJUSTMENT WORKS

There's an important distinction between deductions and adjustments. You cannot deduct fixing-up expenses on your tax return, but you do reduce the taxable gain to the extent of money you spend to sell your house. If you have a small taxable gain this year, fixing-up expenses could help defer part or all of that profit.

EXAMPLE:

The adjusted sales price of your home (sales price less commissions and closing costs) is $92,600. The basis (adjusted purchase price) of the home was $32,000, so your total gain is $60,600. You buy another home for $85,000. Taxable gain this year is $7,600:

Total profit	
Sales price (adjusted)	$92,600
Less: adjusted basis	32,000
Total profit	$60,600
Purchase price, new home	
Sales price (adjusted)	$92,600
Less: purchase price, new home (adjusted)	85,000
Difference	$ 7,600
Deferral of profits	
Profit deferred	$53,000
Profit taxable this year	7,600
Total profit	$60,600

This is the same calculation explained in previous chapters. You are allowed to defer your gain only to the extent that you reinvest in new property. So if you buy or build a house that costs more than the sales price of your present home, the entire gain is deferred. If it costs less, the difference is taxed in the year of sale.

You can reduce the amount you're taxed this year to the extent that you spend money in fixing-up expenses. These include any expenses necessary to get the home ready for sale, such as painting, wallpaper, new carpets and drapes, landscaping, repairs, and replacements. You cannot include capital expenditures (like a new room) as a fixing-up expense.

EXAMPLE:

You plan to sell your house, but it has only one bathroom. Most other homes similar to yours have two baths, so you spend $12,000 to make the addition. This is a capital improvement and cannot be treated as a fixing-up expense. However, it does increase your basis in the house.

Using the previous example, you end up with a taxable gain of $7,600 this year, and can reduce that by the amount spent for fixing-up expenses. So if you spend $2,000 on painting interiors and exteriors, replacing worn windows, adding insulation, and putting in new wallpaper, the taxable portion is reduced:

	Deferred	Taxed
Before fixing-up expenses	$53,000	$ 7,600
Adjusted	+ 2,000	− 2,000
After fixing-up expenses	$55,000	$ 5,600

Figure 25–1 shows the calculations for adjusted sales price.

The fixing-up expenses must be strictly related to your sale. There is also a time limit, both on the performance of work, and on paying for it. You must perform work 90 days or less before the date of sale. And those expenses must be paid for within 30 days after the date of sale (see Figure 25–2).

Many fixing-up expenses are undertaken as part of the negotiation for sale. The buyer requests that minor improvements be made at the time an offer is made. As long as you have a tentative closing date within 90 days, these will qualify as fixing-up expenses. You might lose the adjustment, though, if it takes longer to sell your house.

FIGURE 25–1
Adjusted Sale Price

sale price	$100,000
less: costs	7,400
net sale price	$ 92,600
less: fixing-up expenses	2,000
adjusted sale price	$ 90,600

EXAMPLE:

As part of your plan to put your home on the market, you repaint inside and out, replace carpets and drapes, and spend money on minor repairs. Your real estate broker begins showing the home, and an acceptable offer is made about two months later. However, the sale is not finalized for an additional six weeks. In this case, the fixing-up expenses were performed before the 90-day limit, and cannot be used to adjust the sale price.

MOVING EXPENSES

If you move to a new area, you are entitled to an itemized deduction for the cost of moving. You can deduct the following types of expenses:

1. Transportation of household goods.
2. Expenses of moving from your old residence (including travel and lodging, plus 80 percent of the cost of meals).

FIGURE 25–2
Time Limits

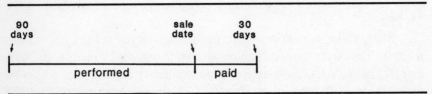

3. Pre-move house-hunting expenses, such as travel, lodging, and 80 percent of meals.
4. Temporary quarters expense, including lodging and 80 percent of meals.

The total of expenses for househunting trips and temporary quarters cannot exceed $1,500. The aggregate total of *all* expenses cannot exceed $3,000 per move, and can be claimed only if you itemize deductions. If you are paying interest on a mortgage, you will probably benefit by itemizing. The cost of moving is split in half if you and your spouse file separate returns. However, if you both move, but to different residences, the total of all moving expenses is doubled to a $6,000 limit.

In addition to these expenses, you are allowed to deduct expenses of selling your old residence, as well as expenses of buying a new one. You can deduct all of the closing costs, both on the sale of your present home and the purchase of a new home as part of your moving expenses. However, you cannot treat these closing costs as moving expenses *and* as adjustments to basis. Renters are allowed to deduct expenses of settling an unexpired lease, and the cost of getting a new lease (but not including refundable deposits).

If you claim moving expenses, the commission and closing costs must be treated either as an adjustment to the deferred gain on sale of your house, or as a deductible moving expense. If you buy another house that costs more than your sales price, it is advantageous to claim a current deduction. But if you have a taxable gain, it makes no difference whether you treat closing costs as a deduction or as an adjustment.

EXAMPLE:

You sell your present house for $115,000, making a profit of $35,000. You move to an area where property values are much lower, and buy a new house for $85,000. You will have a taxable gain of $30,000 this year (the difference between the sales price and the purchase price of the new home).

If you treat closing costs as a moving expense, the adjusted sale and purchase prices will change, and your taxable profit will increase. At the same time, the increase is offset by your itemized deduction.

To qualify for moving expenses, you must meet two tests: one for mileage and one for time. Your new workplace must be at least 35 miles farther from your old residence than your old workplace was. For instance, if you presently commute 20 miles to work, your new job must be at least 55 miles from your previous residence. If it's less, you have not moved far enough to claim any moving expenses.

You can claim moving expenses if you are a full-time employee for no less than 39 weeks during the 12 months following your move. Self-employed people must work at least 39 weeks during the 12 months following the move. They must also work a total of 78 weeks during the 24 months after the move.

EXAMPLE:

You are relocated by your employer. During the following year, you work 49 weeks, and have met the time test.

EXAMPLE:

You are self-employed when you move. During the 12 months after the move, you work 49 weeks. However, in the next 12 months, you only work 25 weeks, or a total of 74 weeks. In this case, you do not qualify for moving expense deduction.

In most cases, you cannot know whether you will meet the time test when you file your tax return. If you expect to, but do not, you must file an amended return and pay an additional tax, using Form 1040-X.

This works in reverse, too. For example, you do not expect to meet the time test, so you don't claim a moving expense deduction. However, you do meet the test, and can file an amended return to claim a refund.

The time test requirement is waived in case of death, disability, or subsequent transfer to another site for the convenience of your employer. And if you are in the armed forces, neither the distance nor time tests are applied when you're transferred to a permanent, new station. If your employer reimburses your moving expenses, you must reduce the claimed expense by the amount of that reimbursement. For more information about moving expenses, get a free copy of *Publication 521, Moving Expenses,* from the IRS. To claim expenses, use Form 3903 (see Figure 25–3).

You may owe taxes because you make a profit from selling your home. However, you are allowed a one-time exclusion of up to $125,000 in profits from a sale. This is the subject of the chapter that follows.

FIGURE 25–3

Form **3903**	**Moving Expenses**	OMB No. 1545-0062

Department of the Treasury
Internal Revenue Service (O)

▶ Attach to Form 1040.
▶ See separate Instructions.

1987
Attachment
Sequence No. **62**

Name(s) as shown on Form 1040   Your social security number

1 Enter the number of miles from your **new** residence to your **new** workplace . . . . | 1 |
2 Enter the number of miles from your **old** residence to your **old** workplace . . . . | 2 |
3 Subtract line 2 from line 1. Enter the result (but not less than zero) . . . . ▶ | 3 |
If line 3 is 35 or more miles, complete the rest of this form. If line 3 is less than 35 miles, you may not take a deduction for moving expenses. This rule does not apply to members of the armed forces.

Part I Moving Expenses

Section A.—Transportation of Household Goods

4 Transportation and storage for household goods and personal effects . . . . | 4 |

Section B.—Expenses of Moving From Old to New Residence

5 Travel and lodging **not** including meals . . . . | 5 |
6 Total meals . . . . | 6 |
7 Reimbursements for meals on line 6 on which no income tax was withheld (see **Meal Expenses** in the Instructions). Do not enter more than the amount shown on line 6 . . | 7 |
8 Subtract line 7 from line 6 . . . . | 8 |
9 Multiply line 8 by 80% (.80) . . . . • . . | 9 |
10 Add lines 5, 7, and 9 . . . . | 10 |

Section C.—Pre-move Househunting Expenses

11 Travel and lodging **not** including meals . . . . | 11 |
12 Total meals . . . . | 12 |
13 Reimbursements for meals on line 12 on which no income tax was withheld (see **Meal Expenses** in the Instructions). Do not enter more than the amount shown on line 12 . . | 13 |
14 Subtract line 13 from line 12 . . . . | 14 |
15 Multiply line 14 by 80% (.80) . . . . | 15 |
16 Add lines 11, 13, and 15 . . . . | 16 |

Section D.—Temporary Quarters (for any 30 days in a row after getting your job)

17 Lodging expenses **not** including meals . . . . | 17 |
18 Total meals . . . . | 18 |
19 Reimbursements for meals on line 18 on which no income tax was withheld (see **Meal Expenses** in the Instructions). Do not enter more than the amount shown on line 18 . . | 19 |
20 Subtract line 19 from line 18 . . . . | 20 |
21 Multiply line 20 by 80% (.80) . . . . | 21 |
22 Add lines 17, 19, and 21 . . . . | 22 |

Section E.—Qualified Real Estate Expenses

23 Expenses of (check one): **a** ☐ selling or exchanging your old residence; or
b ☐ if renting, settling an unexpired lease . . . . . | 23 |
24 Expenses of (check one): **a** ☐ buying your new residence; or
b ☐ if renting, getting a new lease . . . . . . | 24 |

Part II Dollar Limitations

25 Add lines 16 and 22 . . . . | 25 |
26 Enter the smaller of line 25 or $1,500 ($750 if married, filing a separate return, and at the end of the tax year you lived with your spouse who also started work during the tax year) . . . . | 26 |
27 Add lines 23, 24, and 26 . . . . | 27 |
28 Enter the smaller of line 27 or $3,000 ($1,500 if married, filing a separate return, and at the end of the tax year you lived with your spouse who also started work during the tax year) . . . . | 28 |
29 Add lines 4, 10, and 28. This is your moving expense deduction. **Enter here and on Schedule A (Form 1040), line 19.** (Note: *Any payments your employer made for any part of your move (including the value of any services furnished in kind) should be included on Form W-2. Report that amount on Form 1040, line 7. See Reimbursements in the Instructions.)* . . . . ▶ | 29 |

For Paperwork Reduction Act Notice, see separate Instructions.   Form **3903** (1987)

CHAPTER 26

THE EXCLUSION RULE

One provision in the federal tax laws is especially beneficial to sellers aged 55 or over. You are allowed a once-in-a-lifetime tax exclusion of up to $125,000 in profits, even when you do not replace one home with another.

You can buy and sell a series of homes over your lifetime, profiting on each and deferring the taxes. Then, when you sell your last house (perhaps moving to an apartment or a much smaller, cheaper home), you legally escape taxes on a substantial portion of your profits. To qualify for this benefit, you must have used your home as a principal residence for no less than three of the five years immediately preceding the sale date.

PLANNING THE EXCLUSION

You decide when to use the exclusion. For instance, you are planning to sell your house this year, and move to an apartment. You know the profit will be substantial. You can use the exclusion to avoid taxes, but once that has been done, you cannot use it again. And you cannot split the $125,000 total between two or more homes. Once you elect to avoid tax on a profit—no matter how large or small—you have used up your one-time right.

EXAMPLE:

You are selling your home this year, and you do not plan to buy another one within the two-year deferral limit. You make a profit of $45,000, and decide to use the exclusion. Four years later, you buy another home, eventually selling it and making a profit of $60,000. You cannot exclude that profit, since you have already used your exclusion.

Your sale date must occur after your 55th birthday. So if that date is approaching and you want to use the exclusion, waiting a few months could save thousands of dollars in taxes.

A married couple filing separately can split the exclusion, each claiming $62,500 in the same year. However, the rule restricts splitting the exclusion if you are still legally married as of the sale date. Both must either claim the exclusion, or not claim it at all.

There are cases when timing is critical. A single person is entitled to the full $125,000, but a married couple—even a couple who owns two homes—has the same limitation. If you are planning to marry and both you and your intended spouse own property, selling one or both homes before the marriage could save a lot of money on taxes.

EXAMPLE:

You and your intended spouse both own homes and meet all of the tests for the exclusion. You are both over age 55, have not claimed the exclusion before, and have used each home as a principal residence for at least three of the last five years.

Your plan is to sell both homes after the wedding, and buy a condominium. If you do this and make a profit on both homes, you will be limited to only one exclusion, as a married couple.

A second possibility is that one of you sells your home before getting married, and claims the exclusion. You will then change the ownership registration on the remaining home. But in this case, you lose the right to avoid future taxes. When one spouse has previously used the exclusion, it cannot be claimed again on jointly owned property.

The third plan calls for each of you to sell your property *before* the marriage. You are then both entitled to an exclusion up to $125,000 in profit. You then purchase the condominium jointly. This is the best way to maximize the tax advantage of the exclusion rule.

In situations where unmarried people own property together, the exclusion and qualifying rules apply to each owner individually. For instance, two people own property: one is over 55 and the other is under 55. Upon sale, the qualifying person can use the exclusion, while the other must pay tax on their share of the gain (or, they can defer profits by buying another home within two years).

THE REDUCED BASIS

The exclusion is claimed by filing Form 2119, Sale or Exchange of Principal Residence. The election can later be revoked by filing an amended tax return, Form 1040-X.

EXAMPLE:

You claim the exclusion because you do not intend to buy another home. But you later change your mind, buy a house, and qualify for deferral of profits. You can revoke the once-in-a-lifetime exclusion previously claimed, by filing an amended Form 2119.

The amount of profit on a sale is reduced by the $125,000 exclusion you claim. It also affects the basis of a new home.

EXAMPLE:

You make a substantial profit on the sale of a previous home, and buy a smaller home in a different area, for much less money. You use the $125,000 exclusion, in addition to deferring part of your gain:

Sales price, old home		$245,000
Less: basis		40,000
Profit		$205,000
Sales price, old home		$245,000
Less: one-time exclusion		125,000
Adjusted sale price		120,000
Less: price of new home		85,000
Taxable profit		$ 35,000
Price of new home		$ 85,000
Profit on sale	$205,000	
Less: exclusion	125,000	
Less: taxable profit	35,000	
Net total		$ 45,000
Adjusted basis, new home		$ 40,000

In this case, the total gain on the sale of a previous home is broken down into these groups:

Excluded from tax	$125,000
Deferred	45,000
Taxable this year	35,000
Total	$205,000

At the same time, the adjusted basis in your new home is deferred to the extent of nontaxable profits. So when you sell that home, the difference between the sale price and $40,000 will be taxable (or again deferred, if you buy another home within two years from the date of sale).

The total tax savings is significant. For instance, if you pay federal income tax at the rate of 33 percent, you will save more than $56,000:

	33% tax
Total profit from sale	$67,650
Taxable portion, $35,000	11,550
Amount saved	$56,100

In situations where the exclusion rule is not complicated by marriage, divorce, or the purchase of a less expensive home, deferral is a simpler matter.

EXAMPLE:

You bought your first home many years ago for $29,500, and finally sold it for $107,500. The home you own now cost $110,000, and you sold it this year for $144,000. Total profit (including the deferral of previous gains) comes to $112,000. As long as you meet the qualifications for the exclusion rule, none of this gain will be taxable (see Figure 26–1).

TAX FREE OWNERSHIP

You can own several homes, sell each one at a profit, and still never have to pay any income tax. This is due to the combination of the deferral rule and the once-in-a-lifetime exclusion.

Keeping in mind that you cannot defer profits more often than once every two years, you could buy and sell a series of homes and, after age 55, use your exclusion:

	Home #1	*Home #2*	*Home #3*	*Home #4*
Purchase price	$22,000	$ 88,000	$110,000	$140,000
Deferred gain	—	63,000	80,000	95,000
Adjusted basis	$22,000	$ 25,000	$ 30,000	$ 45,000
Sale price	85,000	105,000	125,000	170,000
Profit	$63,000	$ 80,000	$ 95,000	$125,000
Exclusion				125,000
Taxable portion				$ 0

Of course, in this example, the exclusion is exactly the same amount as the adjusted profit, including deferred profits on three previous homes.

FIGURE 26–1
The Exclusion Rule

FIRST HOME	
adjusted sale price	$107,500
less: adjusted basis	29,500
profit	$ 78,000
SECOND HOME	
adjusted purchase price	$110,000
less: deferred profit	78,000
adjusted basis	$ 32,000
adjusted sale price	$144,000
less: adjusted basis	32,000
taxable gain	$112,000
less: exclusion	125,000
amount taxed	$ 0

The point is you can own real estate used as your principal residence, trade up an indefinite number of times, and defer all profits. Then, after age 55, you can exclude a substantial portion of your gain, often the entire amount.

Before deciding to use the exclusion, be sure to compare the benefits to your future needs. If you expect a larger profit in later years, you might be better off paying taxes today and using the exclusion for the next sale. To properly plan ahead and make the right decision, check with your tax adviser.

The question of where to move is discussed in the next chapter. Once you complete your role as a seller, you will again become a buyer. As part of the comprehensive selling process, you must also look ahead and plan with a buyer's point of view.

CHAPTER 27

BUYING A NEW HOME

Once you sell your home, you change roles and become a buyer. But you have a different point of view now than you had the first time around. You already know what it's like to own your own home.

There are other differences, too. You have a sum of money available, perhaps a very large sum. If you lived in your previous home for many years and paid down the morgage loan, equity has built up. And if property values have increased over time, you will receive yet more money for your equity. You will have less trouble qualifying for a loan, and also the choice of putting down more than the standard 20 percent on your new home purchase.

EVALUATING YOUR CHOICES

These factors broaden your choices. First-time buyers often have to take whatever they can afford—lower-priced homes, the fixer-uppers, and homes in areas not as desirable as expected. Now, as a second-time buyer with money in hand, you can probably choose from a much larger group of available properties. Remember these important buying points:

1. *Know how much space you need.* If you are moving because you need a larger home, be sure you specify to a real estate broker how much space you need. And if you are selling because your children have grown up and you no longer need a large home, be equally clear about what you need and want.

2. *Identify a price range.* Before looking for a new home, identify a price range as narrow as possible that you can afford to pay. You know by now approximately how much cash you will have available, allowing for closing and moving costs. Depending on how much you will put down on a new home, and how much you are willing to pay on a mortgage loan each month, you should be able to define in advance what your new home should cost.

3. *Pick the right area.* Evaluate different neighborhoods and pick the one that best suits you. Apply the same standards to evaluation of neighborhoods that you used to test the marketability of your previous home. Look for signs of transition, conveniences, number of homes for sale and sold in recent months, crime statistics, and so forth.

4. *Shop for the right broker.* You also know by now that the broker works for the seller, in the sense that commissions are paid out of sale proceeds. However, a good broker also works for the buyer, making the best match possible between the two sides. Shop around and work with a broker who understands exactly what you're looking for. Don't fall into the trap of selecting a broker at random, or letting someone show you every house on the market, whether or not it suits you.

You will save precious time and energy if you know in advance how much space you need, the price you'll pay, and the area where you want to live. These points eliminate most of the questions a broker will ask. And by working with the right broker—a professional who knows the market and can find what you want—you can cut weeks, even months out of the search.

THE DOWN PAYMENT

If you do have a large sum of money as proceeds from the sale of your present house, you must decide how much you will reinvest in your new home. Some points to keep in mind:

1. The larger the down payment, the smaller your monthly loan payments will be.
2. By putting down more than 20 percent, you could afford a shorter term mortgage. Equity will build more quickly, and you will be able to pay off the loan in a much shorter period of time.
3. The money you put into a down payment is literally invested in your new home. Since it is less available, it is probably safer than it would be in a savings account.
4. You can put a minimum down payment on your new house, and invest part of your proceeds elsewhere. But few, if any, outside investments will yield as much, for as little risk, as your own house.

If you finance your new home, you must be willing to shoulder the inevitable cost of borrowing money. Over a 30-year period, interest more than doubles the cost of your home when you make a 20 percent down payment. This means that, even if your new home doubles in value, the lender receives most or all of the appreciation, through interest on your loan. A large part of the appreciation on your first home probably went to your lender, and the cash you have upon sale is, in reality, a savings account you built up over the years. It can be different this time, though. With a little planning, *you* can benefit from the appreciating value of real estate.

Compare the cost of borrowing, shown in Figure 27–1, for a 30-year loan and a 15-year loan with 20 percent down, 50 percent down, or by paying all cash.

EXAMPLE:

You bought your first home 15 years ago, paying $32,500. You have just accepted an offer for $145,000. After paying off the balance of your mortgage, commission and other closing costs, and paying for your move, you will receive about $110,000.

You plan to buy a home in another area, where average prices are much lower. You can afford a comparable home for about $100,000. If you make an all-cash offer, all future appreciation is yours.

You might be tempted to keep part of the proceeds and invest in some way. You should realize that this is no different than borrowing money secured by home equity; the risks are just as great.

FIGURE 27–1
The Cost of Borrowing

30-YEAR LOAN	$100,000 LOAN, 10%		
	20% DOWN	50% DOWN	ALL CASH
down payment	$ 20,000	$ 50,000	$100,000
financed	80,000	50,000	0
interest	172,742	107,964	0
total cost	$272,742	$207,964	$100,000
15-YEAR LOAN			
down payment	$ 20,000	$ 50,000	$100,000
financed	80,000	50,000	0
interest	74,744	46,716	0
total cost	$174,744	$146,716	$100,000

EXAMPLE:

Instead of moving, you plan to stay where you are. You have about $130,000 in equity in your home, and a lender will gladly loan you up to $100,000. As a homeowner, are you willing to go into debt to free up money to invest? If so, you obligate yourself to monthly payments, and you will be putting your money at risk.

Most homeowners would quickly reject the idea of borrowing to take risks in investments. But upon selling their homes, many people do just that. Recognize that a mortgage loan is borrowed money.

The choice is a clear one. Either reinvest all your equity in your new home, or keep part of it to use in some other way, going into debt in the process. But before you decide to invest, ask yourself this question:

Where can I invest my money so that it will yield a profit, for as little risk as I have in my own home?

Real estate appreciation over a period of years is dependable and consistent. The demand for real estate varies by area and economic conditions, but over the long term, it is a constant. Market values appreciate. If you select a well-constructed home in a good neighborhood, and care for it, your investment will pay off.

Owning and living in your own home makes it an exceptionally good investment. Because you are on site everyday, you maintain it, preserve it, and build market value. You do not have that opportunity with any other type of investment.

Finally, you must compare your home to other investments realistically, with tax considerations in mind.

THE TAX QUESTION

A common argument against paying all cash for a home, or even putting down more than 20 percent, is a tax argument. Many financial advisers say:

Put the minimum down on your new home and invest the rest of the money in something else. This gives you leverage. And by financing your home purchase, you can write off the interest on your tax return. You can't afford to give up that advantage.

This is a flawed argument. Let's assume that your new home will appreciate in value by only 4 percent per year, and that current mortgage interest rates are about 10 percent. A comparison of the first year's interest cost and tax benefits will show why you're better off putting your proceeds into your new house.

If you buy a $100,000 house and make a 20 percent down payment, your 30-year, 10 percent loan will cost you about $7,977 in interest for the first year. On a 15-year loan, the interest will be about $7,892. Figure 27–2 shows the aftertax cost of interest, assuming you pay taxes at the rate of 33 percent.

With a 30-year mortgage, your aftertax interest cost is $5,345. To match this, you will have to earn no less than 17.25 percent with an outside investment. For instance, you invest your $80,000 proceeds at 17.25 percent:

First-year return	$13,800
Less 33% tax	4,554
Aftertax profit	$ 9,246

How does this compare to putting the entire $100,000 into your new house?

Savings on interest after taxes	$ 5,345
4% annual appreciation	4,000
Total profit	$ 9,345

FIGURE 27–2
Tax Advantages

tax advantages

$80,000 LOAN AT 10%	30 YEARS	15 YEARS
interest, first year	$7,977	$7,892
tax reduction (33%)	2,632	2,604
aftertax interest cost	$5,345	$5,288

The comparative return on keeping the money in your own home is valid, for two reasons:

1. You must compare the all-cash purchase to the aftertax cost of borrowing. In this case, with the tax advantages considered, you save $5,345 by not financing any part of your home.

2. The 4 percent annual appreciation assumed on the investment in your home is not taxed. This equity is real, but you are penalized only when selling your home and not buying another one within two years.

The next part of the comparison is to ask yourself where you could invest your money to earn 17.25 percent. This is a very high rate of return in any investment, and it must be earned not just once, but as long as you would be in debt on a mortgage loan.

Remember that if you have to go into debt to invest—as you do if you finance part of your home—you must be able to earn a comparative rate of interest. This example showed what's required just to break even. There's no advantage with the outside investment, even if find one yielding a high rate of return.

You must also consider the difference in your personal budget. When you pay all cash for your new home, you do not have to make a mortgage payment every month. Money is freed up to improve your lifestyle, or to accumulate a retirement or investment fund over time.

Interest on your home mortgage is fully deductible, so it does reduce your tax liability. But don't let that obscure the facts. You're better off with a *smaller* deduction and less interest, than you are with a *larger* deduction and more interest. This is true, no matter what your effective tax rate might be. Always compare the alternatives on an aftertax basis. You will quickly realize that paying a higher amount of interest just for tax purposes is no benefit at all.

A final question to consider is the risk factor. Let's assume that a financial adviser convinces you that it is possible to earn a 17.25 percent rate of return. What about the degree of risk?

When your money is invested in your own home, you have very little risk. You are protected by your homeowner's insurance policy against unexpected catastrophic losses. You aren't depending on a tenant to care for your property, as you're there yourself everyday. And you know that, over many years, your property will increase in value.

How much direct control will you have over an outside investment? Chances are, very little. In order to earn 17.25 percent or more, you have to be willing to live with a higher-than-average risk. There's also a chance you'll lose money on the investment.

The popular arguments favoring leverage and "putting your money to work," while borrowing as much as possible, simply don't work when they're compared to paying for your home in cash.

Avoiding debt on your new home is not always possible. If you must pay off a large mortgage, for example, you will not get as much cash back when you sell. And if you buy a larger home, you will probably have to pay more for it. In these instances, you can reduce the cost of interest by taking out a 15-year loan instead of the more expensive 30-year mortgage.

Upon moving, it's also a good idea to maintain a reasonable cash reserve, even if you didn't have one before. There are inevitably unexpected expenses involved with a move, such as higher relocation costs, a greater amount of income taxes, or a delay in finding a job in your new area. So you might want to keep part of your proceeds to take care of these expenses.

The question of what to do with the proceeds from your sale is different if you do not plan to buy another house. The idea of giving up home ownership and becoming a renter is explored in the next chapter.

CHAPTER 28

BECOMING A RENTER

After you sell your house, you do not have to buy another home. You have the choice of renting an apartment or house, and using the proceeds from your sale to invest. However, before deciding to give up home ownership, compare renting to owning with all expenses in mind.

The comparison is not a simple one. Many of the real advantages of home ownership are intangible. The personal satisfaction, security, and freedom you enjoy as an owner cannot be reduced to a monetary value. And, as many previous homeowners have discovered, renting is far more restrictive than owning.

With these intangible differences in mind, you might still want to rent, as a practical matter. For example, you are selling your large home because you do not need much space any longer. Your children have grown, and the annual cost of insurance, maintenance, utilities, and taxes are too high. As a renter, or as owner of a smaller house, your costs would be lower.

You might find, however, that smaller homes are scarce, or that the price is nearly as high as prices of much larger homes. If the value of land accounts for a large portion of property values in your area, chances are you will pay a premium for even a very small house.

DECIDING TO RENT

In the circumstances just described, renting might be a practical alternative. If you manage your money carefully, you could even pay for part or all of your rent from investment income.

EXAMPLE:

You own your present home free and clear, and are thinking of becoming a renter. You calculate the amount of interest you'll be able to earn each year.

Estimated proceeds after commissions and closing costs will be

$85,000. If that money is put into a savings account at 6.5 percent, you will earn about $5,525 per year, or an average of $460 per month.

In comparison to owning, this might be a less expensive way to go. If rents average $500 per month, you will have to pay out only $40. How does this compare to the cost of maintenance, insurance, utilities, and property taxes? You can save a lot of money each month by becoming a renter. There are a few problems with this plan, however:

1. *Ready cash is tempting.* You might discover that having a large amount of ready cash is too tempting for you. When it's tied up in equity, it's not available. But in a passbook savings account, you know you can withdraw it any time you want. That trip to Europe, a new car, and other expenses are finally affordable.

If you do take part of your proceeds for such expenses, you reduce your monthly interest, and increase the out-of-pocket expense of renting.

2. *Annual income taxes.* The interest you earn on your savings account will be taxable each year. So your estimate of actual cash in hand must be reduced by the amount of taxes you'll have to pay. Also, the rent you pay is not tax deductible. There is no tax advantage to renting.

3. *Taxes on proceeds.* If you do not buy or build another home within two years, the profit you make from selling will be taxed. You could use your one-time exclusion of up to $125,000 if you have not used it before, and if you are age 55 or over.

If you do not qualify for the exclusion, don't count on being able to save all of your proceeds. First calculate how much tax you will owe on your profits.

EXAMPLE:

One homeowner purchased a home 15 years ago for $30,000. Today, it is worth $125,000. But because the homeowner is not yet 55, proceeds will be taxed if another home is not bought. At the rate of 33 percent, taxes on a profit of $95,000 are $31,350—more than the original cost of the house.

4. *Lack of appreciation.* Leaving equity invested in a house will prove to be a good investment over time, assuming property values increase. And if you are able to keep all of your proceeds in a savings account, compound interest will also increase the value of your savings.

Your plan, though, is to withdraw interest to subsidize rent expense. When you do this, you do not benefit from appreciation; the fund will never grow in value.

5. *Rent increases.* Renters live with the constant threat of increases in the cost of housing. They are at the mercy of the supply and demand cycle, and an increase in demand usually means an increase in rent.

6. *Uncertainty about where you'll live.* If rent is increased beyond your ability to afford it, or if the owner of your apartment decides to convert units to condominiums, you will be forced to move. As a homeowner, the choice was yours. As a renter, you will probably move more frequently.

THE TOTAL COMPARISON

If you have enough cash to buy a new home without a mortgage, or if your mortgage will be a small one, owning is definitely advantageous. However, if you plan to mortgage the entire house, the comparison is more complicated.

EXAMPLE:

You are about to sell the house you've owned for five years. With minimal appreciation during the time you owned, you have only enough equity to make a 20 percent down payment on your new home (with all costs considered).

In your area, rents average $500 per month. You estimate that you'll need an $80,000 mortgage loan if you buy, and that the interest rate for a 30-year term will be 10 percent. You also figure out the average monthly cost of property taxes, maintenance, insurance, and utilities. Finally, you adjust the total for the tax advantages of deducting interest and property taxes.

Figure 28–1 shows this cost comparison. On an aftertax basis, owning a home costs $741 per month, while renting is cheaper by $186 per month. This is based on the assumption that your loan will be for $80,000, at 10 percent for 30 years. The tax advantages—based on a rate of 33 percent—are for the first year only. During that first year, total mortgage payments include $7,976 in interest (only $448 goes to principal). Interest expense declines each year you pay on a mortgage. Interest plus property taxes total $8,576; 33 percent of that is $2,830; and one twelfth of that is $236.

At first glance, renting is less expensive and seems to make more sense. There are no property taxes or maintenance expenses; and in-

FIGURE 28–1
Cost Comparison

	RENTING	OWNING
monthly payments	$500	$702
property taxes	0	50
maintenance	0	100
insurance	25	50
utilities	30	75
total cost	$555	$977
tax savings	0	236
aftertax cost	$555	$741

surance and utilities cost much less. But don't overlook the intangible benefits of home ownership, and don't limit the comparison to today's values.

You must compare cost and value in 5 and 10 years. Based on what you believe the percentage of inflation will be, figure out how much rents will increase. Also calculate the potential appreciation in the value of a house.

To figure inflation, add "1" to the rate you assume, and multiply that by the current cost or value. For example, if you assume 4 percent annual inflation, you must multiply today's rent by 1.04:

$$1.04 \times \$555 = \$577$$

This, on average, will be your rent cost for the second year. For the third year, multiply $577 by 1.04. Even if you sign a lease on a rental, you will still be penalized over the long term. Upon expiration of the lease, rents will probably be increased, and inflation is the best estimate of how much increase you should expect.

The same calculation should be applied to housing values. After one year, a $100,000 house will be worth $104,000, at 4 percent inflation. These comparisons are averages, and won't necessarily reflect actual market values. For instance, in your area there could be a low demand for homes, but a very high demand for rental units. In that case, the actual market demand will make a one-to-one comparison invalid.

Figure 28–2 shows how cost and value change over 5 and 10 years,

FIGURE 28–2
Future Cost and Value

	COST OF RENTING	VALUE OF OWNING
today's cost	$555	
today's value		$100,000
4% INFLATION		
5-year change	$675	$121,665
10-year change	822	148,024

assuming the inflation rate is identical for both rentals and home values. If you are considering becoming a renter, you should also consider the future. Rents will increase, so your cost of housing will go up. At the same time, the investment value of home ownership cannot be overlooked. For a fixed monthly housing expense (assuming you finance your purchase with a fixed-rate mortgage), the value of your home will grow over time.

The comparison is much more than just the cost of a mortgage and the cost of monthly rent. There are other costs, tax benefits, and most important of all, the difference in lifestyle and personal freedom, to consider.

Alternatives to selling your house are presented in the next chapter. You can convert equity or turn your house into an investment property, rather than placing it on the market.

CHAPTER 29

ALTERNATIVES TO SELLING

Most people sell their homes because they need to increase their living space, or because they are moving to a new area. But some people sell because they want to cash in their equity. If this is your motive, you face a different dilemma.

As long as we live, we need shelter. And while you are moving from one place to another, you will reinvest equity. Of course, you can trade in a large home for a smaller one. Or you can move to a different region of the country, where housing values are much lower. Beyond these circumstances, however, you will have to contend with the all too common dilemma of the cash-poor but property-rich homeowner. People approaching retirement age often find that they cannot easily cash in on the value they have built up in property over their lives.

About 7 of every 10 people over the age of 65 own their homes, and 84 percent of this group have paid off their mortgage balances. Yet, about two thirds have minimum annual incomes—a combination of social security and a small employer-provided pension.

THE REVERSE ANNUITY MORTGAGE

The problem for retiring homeowners is that, if they sell their homes, they must live somewhere else. And if they borrow money, they must make monthly payments they cannot afford.

One possible solution is the reverse annuity mortgage (RAM). This is a plan sold by some insurance companies, combining annuity benefits and a mortgage loan. Most annuities work in this way: An individual makes payments to the insurance company, either in a lump sum or over a period of years. Then, upon retirement, the insurance company makes monthly annuity payments to the individual. With a RAM, the insurance company begins payments, and each payment adds to an ever growing mortgage debt. This debt will eventually be repaid when your home is sold, which occurs after a specified number of years, or upon the death of the homeowner, depending on the RAM agreement.

In this way, equity is gradually converted from the homeowner to the insurance company. You do not have to make monthly payments against the loan until the annuity period has expired. The amount of monthly benefit you will receive depends on three factors:

1. The current market value of your home.
2. Your age.
3. The number of years of the RAM contract.

Insurance companies that offer RAMS usually make them available only to people aged 62 or older. For example, based on the three factors, you receive $400 per month under a RAM contract. You are given a check each month, which is added to a growing mortgage. The agreed-upon mortgage rate is 11 percent. Figure 29–1 shows how this monthly payment accumulates as a mortgage.

One problem with the RAM is that you might outlive the annuity period. In that case, all of your equity will be gone, and you'll be forced to sell your home, leaving you no shelter. Certain RAM agreements call for payments to continue for the rest of your life, which is a better alternative.

Another problem is that few insurance companies offer RAM contracts, and only in a few states. To find out whether any insurers in your

FIGURE 29–1
Reverse Annuity Mortgage

MONTH	MONTHLY ANNUITY	11% INTEREST	MORTGAGE BALANCE
1	$400.00	$ 0	$ 400.00
2	400.00	3.67	803.67
3	400.00	7.37	1,211.04
4	400.00	11.10	1,622.14
5	400.00	14.87	2,037.01
6	400.00	18.67	2,455.68

state offer reverse annuity mortgages, contact the office of your state insurance commissioner. Also write for free information to the National Center for Home Equity Conversion, 110 East Main, Room 605, Madison, WI 53703.

THE SALE LEASEBACK

Another alternative to outright selling is a plan that not only frees up equity, but ensures that you'll have a place to live—the sale-leaseback. It also helps your grown child to buy real estate. The sale-leaseback, when planned properly, solves a problem for you and your son or daughter. You sell your home to the child, who then rents it back to you. Therefore, you do not have to move.

. From your point of view, the sale-leaseback arrangement frees up a large amount of cash. Upon sale, your child will seek financing from a lender, who will probably advance up to 80 percent of the sales price. You might carry the remaining 20 percent as a personal loan. You will receive the proceeds of the conventional loan (assuming you have no outstanding mortgages of your own). You now become a tenant and your child becomes a landlord. You make monthly rent payments, and your child is responsible for repaying the mortgage to the outside lender, as well as the loan from you.

If you have enough equity built up in your home, the interest on your lump sum should be enough for your rent payments. And for your child, the monthly receipt of rent helps reduce the burden of mortgage payments. As a landlord, your child also has tax benefits through depreciation and the legal deductions of insurance, maintenance, interest, and taxes.

Experts warn that a sale-leaseback must be properly put together, or the Internal Revenue Service could disallow the tax benefits that make it so attractive. The following rules should be observed:

1. Be sure you enter a written lease, using the advice of an accountant or tax attorney.
2. Both you and your child must write out separate checks each month. Yours is for rent payments; your child's is for repayments on the loan you carry. Don't net out the difference. These are two separate transactions, and must be treated accordingly.

3. Rent must be set at a fair market rate, based on rentals for similar homes in your area.
4. The lease must ensure you that you will have a place to live for the indefinite future. So be sure to write in renewal options for yourself.

Upon sale, you can probably escape taxes on your profits by using the one-time exclusion up to $125,000. Little or none of your proceeds will go to taxes. The sale-leaseback can create positive cash flow for you.

EXAMPLE:

You receive $100,000 in cash (when your child takes out a conventional loan, and the proceeds are paid to you, as seller). Your child also makes a 20 percent down payment at the time of purchase. You use the proceeds to purchase a life annuity. At age 65, you will receive about $600 per month. As long as the fair market rent is below $600, you will have money left over after paying rent.

For your child, the monthly rent income can be applied toward mortgage payments, and the tax benefits make the transaction worthwhile as an investment. The child is a landlord, but knows the tenants will care for the property well. And eventually, the child will own the home free and clear.

There are two parts to the sale-leaseback arrangement. First is the sale transaction. Your child must obtain a loan and make payments to an outside lender. You might also carry a small portion of the loan, in which case your child also makes payments to you. Second is the lease agreement. You pay monthly rent to your child, the landlord (see Figure 29-2).

BECOMING A LANDLORD

A third alternative is to move to a smaller house or condominium, and keep your present home as a rental property. This enables you to free up equity to a degree, and to pay your mortgage loan with rental receipts.

EXAMPLE:

Your house is currently valued at about $100,000, and you owe no money to lenders. You can move to smaller, less expensive quarters and rent out your house. At the same time, you borrow $80,000, at 11 percent interest and a 30-year term. Your monthly payments will be $762. If you can rent

FIGURE 29–2
Sale and Leaseback

HOME SALE

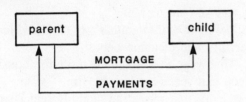

LEASE

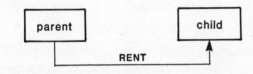

out the house for more than this amount, you can afford the monthly payments. There are considerable risks to this approach:

1. The demand for rental homes could change, and your monthly income could stop.
2. You could have a tenant who is late with rent payments, or stops making them altogether. Not only will you have to evict, but you must also continue your mortgage payments without offsetting income.
3. Unexpected maintenance expenses will create additional cash demands.

Landlording has its own special risks, and you should enter into a rental agreement only after researching it thoroughly. Be sure you understand the risks, and are completely familiar with local laws regarding landlords' and tenants' rights. You should also have money in reserve for unexpected vacancies, maintenance expenses, and possible delays in monthly rent receipts.

Be sure to ask for and check references from anyone to whom you are considering renting your house. Also draw up a written lease or rental agreement, using an attorney's help. Don't depend on a standard lease form. Be sure to include these provisions:

1. The exact due date and amount of rent.
2. Initial payments, including an extra month's rent (first and last), and a refundable security and cleaning deposit.
3. Term of the lease. One year is a standard term for housing rentals. However, you can specify a longer term.
4. Increases. Include a clause that raises the monthly rent if your property taxes or insurance rates are raised.
5. Maintenance. Specify who is responsible for what. Your lease can make the tenant responsible for ongoing routine maintenance of the property, while you agree to take care of major repairs as needed.

The lease should be as specific as possible, covering every possible contingency. As a landlord, you can protect your rights through a lease, to a degree. Beyond that, you must be willing to live with the inconvenience of a tenant calling you on weekends and evenings, demanding that leaky faucets and stuck doors be fixed immediately.

Do not overlook the financial risks. You must be able to afford the possibility that you won't receive rent income for several months. If your tenant fails to make payments, it might take time to evict. And if a slow market means a long vacancy, you must be able to afford to continue your mortgage payments.

Many people have found tenants who take excellent care of their property, pay the rent on time; and never pester the owner. If you can find such a situation, you will enjoy your landlord experience. But the opposite can occur, too—tenants who depreciate your home, don't make payments, and demand constant care and attention. The way you perceive landlording will depend largely on the type of tenant you get. That's why a thorough check of references is essential.

BORROWING EQUITY

If you reject the notion of renting out your house, or do not want a RAM or sale-leaseback arrangement, you probably have to accept the inevitable: You must convert equity rather than "taking it out."

Many lender ads make the statement that your equity is sitting idle in your home, and that it should be put to work. Financial advisers also encourage clients to leverage (borrow) as much as possible, to free up money to invest elsewhere. But remember that all of this advice comes from those who earn money through interest or commissions.

You can never truly "take out" your equity unless you no longer need to pay for shelter. If your grown children offer you a free house, if you're content to become a renter, or if you trade in property ownership for a mobile home, you can take out all of your equity. But most of us move not away from property, but from one place to another.

You can borrow money on a fully paid home, but that money has to be repaid. A mortgage is not taking out equity; it's merely borrowing money with your equity pledged as security. It's doubtful that you will be able to use that borrowed money to produce a consistent rate of return that's greater than the interest you pay to the lender—even after taxes. And even if you can, you will inevitably be taking much greater risks than you have as a homeowner.

Whether you decide to sell and move, become a renter, or take one of the more unusual routes (like a RAM or sale-leaseback), you will still need shelter. Real estate is historically a sound investment. The purpose in selling your home should govern the way you proceed. Don't be swayed by promises of tax advantages, high returns from outside investments, or immediate profits from selling your home.

Always make a clear distinction between personal assets—your family's shelter—and investment property. The more information you have when you sell, the greater your chances for success from your decision. The people who lose money or regret their decision to sell are those who acted on impulse rather than on knowledge.

Explore the alternatives, investigate the facts, and work with qualified professionals. You will then be assured of enjoying the benefits of buying, holding, and eventually selling your home.

GLOSSARY

A

abstract of title   A document that describes the ownership of real estate, including all mortgages and other liens outstanding.

acceptance   Agreeing to the terms of an offer, a necessary act to entering a contract.

addition   The addition of living space, that will increase the market value of property.

adjusted basis   The cost of a home, plus closing costs paid at the time of purchase, plus the cost of improvements, and less any depreciation claimed.

adjusted sales price   The agreed-upon price at the time of sale, less commissions and other closing costs paid by the seller.

affidavit of title   A written statement from the seller, declaring that he or she is the owner of the property, and that no undisclosed mortgages or other liens exist.

aftertax cash flow   The amount of cash received by a landlord or investor, after payment of all mortgages, operating expenses, and taxes.

aftertax profit   The profit from investing in real estate, allowing for tax liabilities, but not including cash paid to the principal portion of a mortgage loan.

agency   A relationship between two individuals, a principal and an agent. The real estate broker acts as agent to the homeowner (principal) during the time a listing is held.

agent   The person who represents the principal, or a real estate broker's employee.

annuity   The payment of a specified amount of money for a period of years, or for life. The individual pays a sum of money to an insurance company, which then guarantees to make monthly annuity payments.

appraisal   An estimate of current market value of a home by an independent and disinterested third party. Appraisers use one of three methods—cost, income, or market comparison—or a combination of the three.

asked price   The price a seller advertises for a house on the market, often used as the starting point in a negotiated offer.

assumable mortgage   A mortgage currently owed by the seller, that can be taken over by a buyer, usually for the same terms and interest rate.

assumption fee   A fee charged by the lender at the time property is transferred, for the administrative costs of transferring the debt.

attorney fees   Fees paid as closing costs for consultation, advice, or escrow services in connection with the sale of real estate.

B

basis   The cost of property, plus closing costs paid at the time of purchase.

before-tax cash flow   The amount of cash received by a landlord, net of operating expenses, and before tax liabilities are computed.

bill of sale   A written document that conveys personal property from the seller to the buyer, used when appliances, furniture, and other possessions are sold at the time a home is transferred.

binder   Also called a "binding receipt," an initial contract that accompanies an offer and initial deposit. This agreement serves as a contract until a more detailed contract can be drawn up.

buyer's broker   A real estate agent who represents the buyer rather than the seller.

C

capital improvement   An addition to property that is permanent, as opposed to routine maintenance.

clear title   Title to property that is free of any disputed liens or mortgages, necessary for the transfer of ownership from seller to buyer.

closing costs   Costs charged to buyer and seller for credit investigation, processing of applications, transfer of ownership, recordings, and insurance.

closing date   The date a sale becomes final.

closing statement   A summary of the price, plus or minus all closing costs, payments on previous loans, and the net payment to the seller; or the net amount owed by the buyer.

commission   A percentage of the sales price of a home, paid by the seller to a real estate broker.

conditional sale   Also called contingency sale, an offer made on the basis of another event taking place by a specified date for the offer to be valid, such as the performance of repairs, the sale of another home, or the buyer's ability to qualify for financing.

contract A legal, written agreement between the buyer and the seller, spelling out the price and other terms of the sale.

conversion The transfer of legal ownership from the seller to the owner, or a change from rental to ownership (as when apartments are converted to condominium units).

cost approach One of three methods of appraising property, in which current value is determined by computing the cost to acquire another property of equal value.

counteroffer An offer made in response to an initial offer, when terms are modified to some degree.

D

deed The instrument specifying ownership, used to convey title from seller to buyer.

deferred profit Profit from selling a house that is not taxed in the year of sale. To qualify for deferral, another house of equal or greater value must be bought or built within two years.

depreciation An amount claimed as a noncash deduction, by investors in rental property; or, the physical decline in value of real estate due to wear and tear.

discount broker Also called flat-fee agent, a real estate broker who offers to assist a seller for a flat fee or a percentage far below the typical market rate. In exchange, limited services are provided.

down payment The amount of money the buyer invests at the onset of the purchase. Most lenders require buyers to commit no less than 20 percent of the purchase price, as a down payment.

E

earnest money Describes the initial deposit given at the time a buyer makes an offer to buy property. This is required as a sign that the offer is serious. It is accompanied with a binder or initial contract specifying the purchase price and other terms.

equity That part of a property's value the owner has, computed as the total current market value, less all outstanding mortgages and other secured liens on the property.

equity buildup   The gradual increases in the owner's equity, occurring from three sources: (1) the repayment of mortgage principal; (2) additions made to the property; and (3) increases in market value due to growing demand for housing.

equity conversion   The process that takes place when equity moves from the seller to someone else. Under the terms of a reverse annuity mortgage, for example, the homeowner receives a monthly payment and, in return, gradually converts ownership to an insurance company.

escrow   A period of time between the entering of an agreement, and the actual closing date of the sale. This time is required to conduct a title search, obtain financing for the buyer, and record the sale.

escrow fee   A fee assessed by the escrow agent, against buyer, seller, or both, for the management of funds and paperwork during the escrow period.

exclusion rule   A provision in federal tax law, allowing homeowners aged 55 or older to exclude from taxes up to $125,000 in profits from selling a home.

exclusive listing   A contract between the seller and a real estate broker, giving the broker the exclusive right to sell the home for a specified period of time.

F

firm contract   Any contract that is final and complete, without any outstanding contingencies or conditions.

firm price   Descriptive of an asked price when the seller is not willing to accept a reduced offer.

fixing-up expenses   Expenses performed within 90 days of the closing sale date, and paid for within 30 days after that date, in anticipation of a sale. These expenses reduce the adjusted sales price of the home, for purposes of computing profits and deferral for taxes. However, they are not deductible as current expenses.

free and clear   A property on which there are no outstanding mortgates and liens.

full disclosure   The revealing of all facts and conditions, required in most states. Sellers and real estate brokers must disclose known conditions to the buyer.

G

good faith deposit   A deposit made by the buyer at the time an offer is given to the seller.

H

home inspection An independent inspection of property offered for sale, including a written report on conditions. The purpose of the inspection is to discover and report any defects in the property that the broker and seller must disclose to the buyer.

I

improvement The upgrading of a property's market value, through the addition of living space or other features.

income approach One of three appraisal methods, used primarily for income-producing property. The current market value is based on current and future gross rental receipts, times a multiplier based on the market value of other, recently sold income properties.

inspection clause A provision written into a sale contract, stating that an offer is contingent upon the satisfactory completion of an independent home inspection.

installment sale A sale in which the proceeds will be paid over time, rather than in a lump sum.

L

lease A written agreement between landlord and tenant, specifying the terms of property rental for a period of months or years.

lease with option to buy One method of transferring property. The seller collects monthly rent plus a sum of money that accumulates toward a future down payment. The tenant has the option to either buy the home within a stated period of time, for a fixed price, or to retrieve deposited money and not purchase the house.

legal description A description of property, giving the exact boundaries and location, including references to plat maps.

leverage The use of money to borrow more money, to increase potential income from appreciation.

listing An agreement between the seller and the real estate broker. It may be exclusive, open, or multiple. The agreement spells out the rate of commission the broker will receive from proceeds upon completion of a sale, and the responsibilities of the broker during the term.

listing broker The real estate broker with a listing on a home for sale. In the event another broker finalizes the sale, the selling broker and the listing broker will split the commission.

M

market comparison approach A method of appraisal or of estimating a property's value, based on recent sales prices of similar homes in the same area.

market value The current value of a home, based on the assumption that a seller is willing to leave the home on the market for a reasonable period of time.

meeting of the minds A condition that must exist for a contract to be valid. Both seller and buyer must agree to the terms of the contract, or no contract exists.

mortgage acceleration The repayment of a mortgage loan more rapidly than required by contract. The purpose of acceleration is to reduce the total cost of interest.

N

net listing A type of listing agreement in which the broker receives the difference between the actual sale price and a specified minimum amount the seller desires to receive. Net listings are illegal in most states.

new basis The basis of real estate after adjusting for deferrred profits from the sale of a previous home. The deferral reduces the basis for future tax purposes.

notary fee A closing cost assessed for the notarization of documents in the sale and recording process.

O

offer to purchase An offer made by someone interested in buying real estate from the seller.

offer to sell An offer by the seller, represented by the asked price and listing of the home.

open listing A listing offered through several real estate brokers at the same time, either by use of a Multiple Listing Service (MLS) or some other shared arrangement among the brokers involved.

over improvement Adding to the value of a home beyond the reasonable market value of similar homes in the same area. Market values are limited, to an extent, to the range of recent sale prices of similar homes, so improving beyond this range will not return a profit to the seller. In some cases, the seller might not be able to recover the cost of the improvement.

P

performance A necessary act to make a contract valid. Each side must perform in accordance with the agreement. A seller performs by transferring title and complying with other terms. A buyer performs by paying the price of the home.

personal property Possessions other than real estate, including furniture, appliances, automobiles, and other property not affixed to land or its structures.

prepayments The advance payment of taxes, insurance, or interest, requiring a prorated adjustment between seller and buyer at the time of closing.

principal The individual represented by the agent in an agency relationship. The homeowner is the principal when working with a real estate broker during the time a home is being offered for sale.

principal residence For purposes of qualifying for deferral of profits or for the one-time $125,000 exclusion of profits upon sale, the home that owners occupied for no less than three of the previous five years.

proration The division of prepaid interest, taxes, or insurance between seller and buyer as of the closing date.

R

ready, willing, and able Descriptive of a buyer who is qualified and serious in making an offer on a home. For example, a buyer is not able if he or she cannot qualify for financing.

real estate cycle The changing conditions of supply and demand, affected by interest rates, taxes, population, employment trends, development, and recent prices of homes.

real property Structures permanently attached to land, and the land itself, as well as the intangible rights attached to ownership.

recording fee A closing cost charged for recording the conveyance of property, or for the commitment to a mortgage debt.

replacement cost An appraisal method, in which current value is estimated based on the cost to completely replace the property. The basis depends on the current cost of land, materials, and labor.

reverse annuity mortgage (RAM) An agreement for equity conversion. A homeowner enters into an agreement with an insurance company, under which monthly annuity payments are made to the homeowner. In exchange, the insurance company has the right to recover its investment, plus interest, when the home is sold.

S

sale-leaseback   A method of accessing equity while retaining possession of a home. A parent sells the home to a grown child, who collects monthly rent as the landlord. The sale proceeds are paid to the parent, who then becomes a tenant.

seller takeback   A form of loan carried by the seller. The buyer of the property must make periodic payments, plus interest.

selling broker   The broker who actually finalizes the sale, whether or not this person is the listing broker.

settlement   The finalization of the sale, occuring on the closing date or upon completion of all contingencies and conditions of the contract.

T

tax deferral   A delay in taxation on the profits from selling a home. Taxes are eventually paid when a home is sold and not replaced by another that costs as much or more than the previous one.

termite inspection   An inspection performed by a qualified termite inspector, to determine whether a home is infested with destructive pests.

title   Legal ownership of property.

title insurance   An insurance policy issued by a title company to the owner of real estate, that stays in effect as long as the property is held. It insures the owner against any undiscovered liens or mortgages.

title search   The process of examining the title to a property, to discover any undisclosed mortgages or liens.

U

unilateral listing   A form of listing in which no one broker has an exclusive right to show the property or earn a sales commission.

V

void contract   Any contract that is unenforceable or illegal. If the essential elements of offer and acceptance are not present, or if there is no meeting of the minds, no contract exists.

INDEX